The
Society
of
Individuals

CW00734233

For my friends
Hermann and Elke Korte

Norbert Elias

The Society of Individuals

Edited by Michael Schröter
Translated by Edmund Jephcott

Seedcorn scattered to the winds
Knowledge for whoever finds

CONTINUUM

New York   London

2001

The Continuum International Publishing Group Inc
370 Lexington Avenue, New York, NY 10017

The Continuum International Publishing Group Ltd
The Tower Building, 11 York Road, London SE1 7NX

Copyright © 1991 by Basil Blackwell

First published in German as *Die Gesellschaft der Individuen* by Suhrkamp
Verlag, copyright © The Norbert Elias Stichting 1987

All rights reserved No part of this book may be reproduced, stored in a retrieval
system, or transmitted, in any form or by any means, electronic, mechanical,
photocopying, recording, or otherwise, without the written permission of the
publishers

Library of Congress Cataloging-in-Publication Data

Elias, Norbert
  [Gesellschaft der Individuen English]
  The society of individuals / Norbert Elias , edited by Michael Schroter ,
translated by Edmund Jephcott
      p cm
  Originally published Oxford, UK , Cambridge, Mass   Basil Blackwell,
1991
  Includes bibliographical references and index
  ISBN 0-8264-1372-2 (pbk   alk paper)
  1 Individualism   2 Human beings   3 Self-consciousness   I Schroter,
Michael   II Title
  HM1276 E45 2001
  302 5'4—dc21

                                                        2001037295

Contents

Preface

The relation of the plurality of people to the single person we call the "individual", and of the single person to the plurality, is by no means clear at present. But we often fail to realize that it is not clear, and still less why. We have the familiar concepts "individual" and "society", the first of which refers to the single human being as if he or she were an entity existing in complete isolation, while the second usually oscillates between two opposed but equally misleading ideas. Society is understood either as a mere accumulation, an additive and unstructured collection of many individual people, or as an object existing beyond individuals and incapable of further explanation. In this latter case the words available to us, the concepts which decisively influence the thought and action of people growing up within their sphere, make it appear as if the single human being, labelled the individual, and the plurality of people conceived as society, were two ontologically different entities.

This book is concerned with that to which the concepts "individual" and "society" in their present form refer, that is, with certain aspects of human beings. It offers tools for thinking about and observing people. Some of them are quite new. It is unusual to talk of the society of individuals. But it may be quite useful to be able to emancipate oneself from the older, more familiar

The initiative of Michael Schroter, and collaboration with him, have made possible the appearance of this book in its present, experimental form I should like to express my thanks to him I am also indebted to my assistants Rudolf Knijff and Jan-Willem Gerritsen for their indispensable help

usage, which often makes the two terms look like simple opposites. That is not enough. To liberate thought from the compulsion to understand the two terms in this way is one of the
objectives of this book. It can only be achieved if one goes
beyond a mere negative criticism of the use of the two terms as
opposites, and sets up a new model of the way in which, for good
or ill, individual human beings are bound to each other in a
plurality, that is, a society.

That this is one of the cardinal problems of sociology became
clear to me about fifty years ago, when I was working on my study
The Civilizing Process. In fact, the first sketches of *The Society of
Individuals* were conceived as a part of the comprehensive theory
contained in volume 2 of that book. I still have some proofs of the
book on civilization, the content of which forms part of Part I of
the text published here.

During my work on the earlier book the problem of the
relation of individual and society kept cropping up. For the
civilizing process extended over very many generations; it could
be traced through the observable movement of the threshold of
shame and embarrassment in a specific direction. This meant that
people of a later generation entered the civilizing process in a
later phase. In growing up as individuals they had to adapt to a
later standard of shame and embarrassment, of the whole social
process of conscience-formation, than people of the preceding
generations. The entire stock of social patterns of self-regulation
which the individual has to develop within himself or herself in
growing up into a unique individual, is generation-specific and
thus, in the broader sense, society-specific. My work on the
civilizing process therefore showed me very clearly that something which did not arouse shame in an earlier century could be
shameful in a later one, and vice versa – I was well aware that
movements in the opposite direction were also possible. But no
matter what the direction, the evidence of change made clear to
what extent individual people are influenced in their development
by the position at which they enter the flow of the social process.

After I had worked for some time it became clear to me that

the problem of the relation of the individual to social processes was threatening to dislocate the framework of the book on civilization, despite the close links between the two subjects. The civilization book was long enough in any case. I therefore brought it to a conclusion and extracted from it the attempts to clarify the relation of society and individual which I had already begun. The subject fascinated me. Its importance to the foundations of sociology as a science became increasingly clear to me. I continued to work on it, first producing the text which is printed as the first part of this book. It shows an early stage of my grappling with the problem. But it also shows that an account of a relatively early stage of research on a fundamental problem has a value of its own, even though work on the problem has advanced further.

It is hard not to believe that if the development of more comprehensive, later solutions to a problem is reconstructed by documenting the different stages of research, access to the later stages of the solution will be easier. By being able to think through the limited earlier solutions, the reader is spared the difficulty of trying to understand the later ideas as if they had emerged from nowhere, without prior reflection, in the head of a particular person. Underlying the structure of this book is a quite different conception of how ideas are formed. Its three component parts were written at different times. The first shows the earliest stage of my reflections on the problem of the single person within the plurality of people, the theme announced by the book's title. The second part is an example of later work on the same question; the third is the latest and final stage of this continuing work.

The change in my approach to the problem of the relation of individual and society, which has taken place over a good fifty years, doubtless reflects specific changes that have taken place in individuals and societies in the same period. It thus reflects changes in the way society is understood, and even in the way the individual people forming these societies understand themselves, in short, the self-image and social make-up – what I call the habitus – of individuals. But on the other hand, as we shall see, the whole manner in which the problem is approached has also changed considerably. The problem has become more concrete. The concepts used fit more closely around the observable situation of individual people within society. Paradoxically, this is accompanied by a raising of the discussion towards a synthesis at a higher level. This finds expression in the fundamental concept of the we–I balance, which indicates that the relation of the I-identity to the we-identity of an individual is not fixed once and for all, but is subject to very specific transformations. In small, relatively simple tribes this relation is other than in the large, contemporary industrial states, in peace other than in contemporary wars. The concept opens up questions of the relation of individual and society to discussion and investigation that would remain inaccessible as long as one conceived a person, and therefore oneself, as a we-less I.

Norbert Elias

Part I

The Society of Individuals
(1939)

I

Everyone knows what is meant when the word "society" is used, or at least, everyone thinks he knows. One person passes the word on to another like a coin whose value is known and whose content no longer needs to be tested. If one person says "society" and another hears it, they understand each other without difficulty. But do we really understand each other?

Society, as we know, is all of us; it is a lot of people together. But a lot of people together in India and China form a different kind of society than in America or Britain; the society formed by many individual people in Europe in the twelfth century was different from that in the sixteenth or the twentieth century. And although all these societies certainly consisted and consist of nothing other than many individuals, the change from one form of living together to another was clearly unplanned by any of these individuals. At least, it cannot be discovered that any person in the twelfth or even the sixteenth century consciously planned the development of the industrial society of our day. What kind of a formation is it, this "society" that we form together, which has not been intended or planned by any of us, or even all of us together? It only exists because a large number of people exist, it only continues to function because many individual people want and do certain things, yet its structure, its great historical transformations, clearly do not depend on the intentions of particular people.

In considering the answers given to these and suchlike questions today, one finds oneself confronted, in broad terms, by two large opposed camps. One section of people approaches socio-historical formations as if they had been designed, planned and created, as they now stand before the retrospective observer, by a number of individuals or bodies. Individuals within this general camp may at some level be aware that their kind of answer is not quite adequate. For no matter how they twist their ideas to fit the facts, the conceptual model to which they are tied remains that of the rational and deliberate creation of a work – such as a building or a machine – by individual people. When they have particular social institutions before them, parliaments, police, banks, taxes or whatever they may be, to explain them they look for the people who first created such institutions. If they are dealing with a literary genre, they look for the writer who gave the others a model. When they encounter formations where this kind of explanation is difficult – language or the state, for example – they at least proceed *as if* these social formations could be explained in the same way as the others, the ones deliberately produced by individual people for a specific purpose. They may argue, for example, that the purpose of language is communication between people, or that the purpose of a state is the upholding of order, as if in the course of mankind's history language or the organization of particular associations of people in the form of states had been deliberately created for this specific purpose by individual people as a result of rational thought. And often enough, when confronted by social phenomena that clearly cannot be explained according to this model, for example, the evolution of artistic styles or the civilizing process, their thinking comes to a halt. They stop asking questions.

The opposing camp despises this way of approaching historical and social formations. For them the individual plays no part at all. Their conceptual models are taken primarily from the natural sciences, particularly biology. But here, as so often, the scientific modes of thought easily and imperceptibly merge with religious and metaphysical ones to form a perfect unity. A society is conceived, for example, as a supra-individual organic entity which advances ineluctably towards death through stages of youth, maturity and age. Spengler's ideas are an example, but related notions are to be found today, independently of Spengler, in the most diverse colours and shades. And even if one is not misled by the experiences of our time into forming a general theory of the necessary rise and decline of societies, if one even anticipates a better future for our society, even opponents within the same camp share an approach which tries to explain socio-historical formations and processes by the influence of anonymous, supra-individual forces. Sometimes, most notably in Hegel, this gives rise to a kind of historical pantheism: a World Spirit or even God Himself, so it seems, becomes embodied in a moving historical world, unlike the static one of Spinoza, and serves as an explanation for its order, its periodicity and its purposefulness. Or this kind of thinker at least imagines particular social formations to be inhabited by a common supra-individual spirit, such as the "spirit" of ancient Greece or of France. Whereas for the people of the opposite persuasion individual actions are at the centre of interest and any phenomena that cannot be explained in the manner of something planned and created by individuals are more or less lost to view, here, in the second camp, it is the very aspects which the other camp finds unmanageable – styles and cultural forms or economic forms and institutions – which are given most attention. And whereas in the former camp it remains obscure how a bridge is to be thrown between individual actions and purposes and such social formations, it is no clearer, in the latter camp, how the forces producing the formations are to be linked to the goals and actions of individual people, whether these forces are seen as anonymously mechanical or as supra-individual forces based on pantheistic models.

But difficulties of this kind are not only encountered in studying historical and social facts in the narrower sense. They are no less intrusive when one is trying to understand human beings and society in terms of psychological functions. In the science which deals with facts of this kind one finds on one hand branches of research which treat the single individual as something that can be completely isolated, and seeks to elucidate the structure of its psychological functions independently of its relations to all other people. On the other hand one finds trends in social or mass psychology which give no proper place to the psychological functions of the single individual. Sometimes the members of this latter camp, much like their counterparts in the social and historical sciences, ascribe to whole social formations or to a mass of people a soul of their own beyond the individual souls, an *anima collectiva* or a "group mind". And if they do not go so far, they are usually content to treat socio-psychological phenomena as the sum or, what comes to the same thing, the average of the psychological manifestations of many individuals. Society then appears simply as an additive accumulation of many individuals, and the statistical processing of psychological data not just as an essential aid but as the goal of and the strongest evidence in psychological research. And however the various branches of individual and social psychology may proceed in detail, from this general standpoint the relation between the objects of their study remains more or less mysterious. Often enough it appears as if the psychologies of the individual and of society were two completely separable disciplines. And the questions posed by each are usually framed in such a way as to imply from the outset that an unbridgeable gap exists between the individual and society.

Wherever we look we meet the same antinomies. We have a certain traditional idea of what we ourselves are as individuals. And we have a certain notion of what we mean when we say "society". But these two ideas, the consciousness we have of ourselves as society on one hand and as individuals on the other, never really coalesce. No doubt we realize at the same time that in reality such a gulf between individual and society does not exist. No one can be in doubt that individuals form a society or that each society is a society of individuals. But when we try to reconstruct in thought what we experience each day in reality we find, as with a jigsaw puzzle the pieces of which will not form a whole picture, that gaps and fissures are constantly forming in our train of thought.

What we lack – let us freely admit it – are conceptual models and an overall vision by which we can make comprehensible in thought what we experience daily in reality, by which we could understand how a large number of individuals form with each other something that is more and other than a collection of separate individuals – how they form a "society", and how it comes about that this society can change in specific ways, that it has a history which takes a course which has not been intended or planned by any of the individuals making it up.

Aristotle, in trying to master a similar difficulty, once pointed to a simple example, the relation of stones to a house. This does indeed provide us with a simple model which shows how many individual elements together form a unity the structure of which cannot be inferred from its separate elements. For one certainly cannot understand the structure of the whole house by contemplating in isolation each of the stones which form it. Nor can one understand it by thinking of the house as an additive unity, an accumulation of stones; this may not be quite useless to an understanding of the whole house, but it certainly does not take us very far to make a statistical analysis of the characteristics of the individual stones and then work out the average.

The *Gestalt* theory of our day has probed more deeply into such phenomena. It has first taught us that a whole is different to the sum of its parts, that it embodies laws of a special kind which cannot be elucidated by examining its individual elements. The theory has provided the general consciousness of our time with a number of simple models which can help us to think further in this direction, such as the example of the melody, which also consists of nothing other than individual notes yet is other than their sum, or that of the relation of word to sounds, sentence to words, book to sentences. All these examples show the same thing: the combination, the relationships of units of lesser magnitude or, to use a more precise term from set theory, units of a lower power, give rise to a unit of higher power that cannot be understood if its parts are considered in isolation, independently of their relationships.

But if these are the models which are to facilitate our thinking on the relation of individual and society, no wonder our self-image resists them. The stones that are cut and fitted together to form a house are no more than a means; the house is the end. Are we too, as individual human beings, no more than means which live and love, struggle and die, for the sake of the social whole?

This question leads on to a debate the twists and turns of which are all too familiar to us. One of the great controversies of our time is carried on between those who maintain that society in its different manifestations – the division of labour, state organization or whatever it may be – is only a "means", the "end" being the well-being of individual people, and those who assert that the well-being of individuals is less "important", the more important thing, the "end" of individual life, being the maintenance of the social unit of which the individual is a part. Would it not already be to take sides in this debate if one were to start looking for models for understanding the relation of individual and society in the relationships between bricks and house, notes and melody, part and whole?

In social life today we are incessantly confronted by the question how and whether it is possible to create a social order which would allow a better harmonization of the personal needs and inclinations of individuals on one hand and the demands made on each individual by the collaborative work of many, the maintenance and efficiency of the social whole on the other. There is no doubt that this, the development of society in such a way that not merely a few but all of its members have a chance to attain such harmony, is what we would call into being if our wishes had enough power over reality. But if one thinks calmly on the matter it soon emerges that the two things are only possible together: there can only be a communal life freer of disturbance and tension if all the individuals within it enjoy sufficient satisfaction; and there can only be a more satisfied individual existence if the relevant social structure is freer of tension, disturbance and conflict. The difficulty seems to be that in the social orders which present themselves to us, one or the other always has the worst of it. Between personal needs and inclinations and the demands of social life, in the societies familiar to us, there seems to be always a considerable conflict, an almost unbridgeable gap, for the majority of people involved. And it seems reasonable to suppose that it is here, in these discrepancies in our lives, that the reasons for the corresponding discrepancies in our thought are to be sought. There is clearly a connection between the gaps which open between individual and society, now here, now there, in our thought structures, and the contradictions between social demands and individual needs which are a permanent feature of our lives. The programmes offered to us today for putting an end to these difficulties seem, on close inspection, merely to want to buy one thing at the expense of the other.

The severity of the conflicts which are constantly calling the relation of individual and society into question today confines our thought within certain limits. The agitation and fear which these conflicts stir up in all concerned are seen in the affective charges carried by all words directly or indirectly related to them; they coalesce around such words to form an aura of valuations which obscures rather than illuminates what they are meant to express. Any idea which alludes no matter how remotely to this dispute is unerringly interpreted as taking a position on one side or the other, as either presenting the individual as the "end" and society as the "means", or seeing society as the more "essential", the "highest purpose", and the individual as "less important", a "means". To try to go behind this antithesis or – if only in thought – to break through it, seems meaningless to the participants in the dispute. Here, too, the questions come to a halt at a very specific point: anything which does not serve to justify either society or the individual as the "more important", the "highest purpose", seems irrelevant, not worth the trouble of thinking about. But what if a better understanding of the relation of individual and society could only be attained by breaking through the either/or, melting the frozen antithesis?

By peeling away the layers of disguise concealing the core of the antithesis, we can begin to resolve it. Those who stand opposed to each other here as enemies both speak as if they had received their knowledge from heaven or from a sphere of reason immune to experience. Whether they say society or the individual is the highest purpose, both parties proceed in thought as if a being outside humanity, or its representative within our thought, "nature" and a God-like "reason" which operates before all experience, had set up this final purpose and this scale of values in this form for all time. If we penetrate the veil of valuations and affects with which the tensions of our time imbue everything connected with the relation of individual to society, a different picture emerges. Considered at a deeper level, both individuals and the society they form together are equally without purpose. Neither exists without the other. First of all, they are simply there, the individual in the society of others, society a society of individuals – as purposeless really as the stars which together form a solar system, or solar systems which form a Milky Way. And this purposeless existence of individuals in society with each other is the material, the basic fabric into which people weave the varying figures of their purposes.

For people set themselves different purposes from one case to another, and there are no other purposes than the ones they set themselves. "Society is the final purpose and the individual only a means", "the individual is the final purpose and the union of individuals into a society only a means to his/her well-being" – both are war-cries which hostile groups shout at each other in the context of their present situation with its transient pressures and interests. Both slogans express something which the two groups believe *ought* to be the case. Only if one goes behind the slogans and overcomes the need to proclaim before everyone what the relation between individual and society ought to be if one were to have one's way, only then does one begin to become aware of the more fundamental question as to what in all the world the relation between individual and society actually *is*. How is it possible – this is now the question – that the simultaneous existence of many people, their living together, their reciprocal actions, the totality of their relations to each other, gives rise to something that none of the individuals, considered in isolation, has intended or brought about, something of which he is a part, whether he wishes or not, a structure of interdependent individuals, a society? It might be a good thing that here, as in the case of nature, we can only clarify our actions, our goals and ideas of what ought to be, if we better understand what is, the basic laws of this substratum of our purposes, the structure of the larger units we form together. Only then would we be in a position to base the therapy for the ills of our communal life on a secure diagnosis. Until that is the case we behave in all our deliberations on society and its ills much like quacks in the treatment of illnesses: we prescribe a therapy without having being able first to establish a clear diagnosis independent of our own wishes and interests.

There is no doubt that the individual human being is brought up by others who were there before him; no doubt that he grows up and lives as part of an association of people, a social whole – whatever that may be. But that means neither that the individual is less important than society, nor that he is a "means" and society the "end". The relation of part to whole is a certain form of relationship, nothing more, and as such is undoubtedly problematic enough. It can under certain circumstances be linked to the relation of means to end, but is not identical to it; very often one form of relation has not the slightest connection to the other.

But if one starts in this way to penetrate the fog of extraneous valuations surrounding the relation of individual and society, another problem immediately emerges beyond it. The statement "The individual is part of a larger whole that he forms together with others" does not say much; it is really no more than a very banal and self-evident observation. Or, to be more exact, it *would be* a banal observation if so many people did not constantly fail to register this simple state of affairs. A great many of the statements on the relation of individual and society that we come across today boil down to the opposite idea. "In reality", the exponents of this standpoint think and feel, "there is no such thing as a society; in reality there are only individuals." And those who, in an exact sense of the phrase, fail to see the wood for the trees, might find their thinking somewhat assisted by the allusion to the relation of stones and house, part and whole. The assertion that individuals are more "real" than society is nothing other than an expression of the fact that the people who hold this view believe individuals to be more *important*, and the association they form, the society, less important. The idea that in "reality" there is no such thing as a society, only a lot of individuals, says about as much as the statement that there is in "reality" no such thing as a house, only a lot of individual bricks, a heap of stones.

But in fact allusions to other wholes, to sounds and words, stones and house, are no more than a very rough guide. Strictly speaking, they only show where the problem lies. They provide a starting point from which one can slowly pursue one's ideas, in constant touch with experience. For even if examples like the house may give some help with the first step when thinking about what a "society" is, at the next step the differences only emerge all the more clearly. By a "whole" we generally mean something more or less harmonious. But the social life of human beings is full of contradictions, tensions and explosions. Decline alternates with rise, war with peace, crises with booms. The communal life of human beings certainly is not harmonious. But if not harmonious, at least the word "whole" evokes in us the idea of something complete in itself, a formation with clear contours, a perceptible form and a discernible, more or less visible structure. But societies have no such perceptible form. They do not possess structures that can be seen, heard or touched directly in space. Considered as wholes, they are always more or less incomplete: from wherever they are viewed they remain open in the sphere of time, towards the past and the future. Fathers, the sons of fathers, are followed by sons, mothers by daughters. It is in reality a continuous flow, a faster or slower change of living forms; in it the eye can find a fixed point only with great difficulty.

And even in each present moment, people are in more or less

perceptible motion. What binds the individuals together is not cement. Think only of the bustle in the streets of a large city: most of the people do not know each other. They have hardly anything to do with each other. They push past each other, each pursuing his or her own goals and plans. They come and go as it suits them. Parts of a whole? The word "whole" is certainly out of place, at least if its meaning is determined solely by a vision of static or spatially closed structures, by experiences like those offered by houses, works of art or organisms.

But there is undoubtedly a different side to the picture: at work in this tumult of scurrying people, for all their individual freedom of movement, there is clearly also a hidden order, not directly perceptible to the senses. Each individual person in this turmoil belongs in a particular place. He has a table at which he eats, a bed in which he sleeps; even the hungry and homeless are both products and parts of the hidden order underlying the mêlée. Each of the people who pass has somewhere, at some time, a specific function, property or work, a task of some kind for others, or a lost function, lost possessions and lost work. There are shop assistants and bank clerks, cleaners and society ladies without a profession of their own; there are men who live on interest, policemen, road-sweepers, ruined property speculators, pickpockets and girls with no other function than the pleasure of men; there are paper wholesalers and fitters, directors of a large chemicals concern and the unemployed. As a result of his function each of these people has or had an income, high or low, from which he lives or lived; and as he passes along the street, this function and this income, more openly or more hidden, goes with him. He cannot jump out of it as the humour takes him. He cannot simply switch to another function, even if he wishes to. The paper wholesaler cannot suddenly become a fitter, the unemployed person a factory director. Still less can any of them, even if he wanted to, become a courtier or a knight or a brahmin, except in the wish-fulfilment of a fancy-dress ball. He is obliged to wear a certain form of dress; he is tied to a certain ritual in dealing with others and specific forms of behaviour very different from those of people in a Chinese village or an urban artisans' community in the early Middle Ages. The invisible order of this form of living together, that cannot be directly perceived, offers the individual a more or less restricted range of possible functions and modes of behaviour. By his birth he is inserted into a functional complex with a quite definite structure; he must conform to it, shape himself in accordance with it and perhaps develop further on its basis. Even his freedom to choose among the pre-existing functions is fairly limited. It depends largely on the point at which he is born and grows up within this human web, the functions and situation of his parents and the schooling he receives accordingly. This too, this past, is also directly present in each of the people scurrying about in the city bustle. It may be that the individual does not know anyone in this bustle; somewhere he has people he knows, trusted friends and enemies, a family, a circle of acquaintances to which he belongs or, should he be now alone, lost or dead acquaintances who live only in his memory.

In a word, each of the people who pass each other as apparently unconnected strangers in the street is tied by invisible chains to other people, whether they are chains of work and property or of instincts and affects. Functions of the most disparate kinds have made him dependent on others and others on him. He lives, and has lived since a child, in a network of dependences, that he cannot change or break simply by turning a magic ring, but only as far as their structure itself allows; he lives in a tissue of mobile relationships, which have by now been precipitated in him as his personal character. And this is where the real problem lies: in each association of human beings this functional context has a very specific structure. It is different in a tribe of cattle-rearing nomads than in a tribe of farmers; it is different in a feudal warrior society than in the industrial society of our day, and over and above this it is different in the different national communities of industrial society itself. However, this basic framework of interdependent functions, the structure and pattern of which gives a society its specific character, is not a creation of particular individuals; for each individual, even the most powerful, even a tribal chief, an absolutist monarch or a dictator, is a part of it, the representative of a function which is formed and maintained only in relation to other functions, which can only be understood in terms of the specific structure and the specific tensions of this total context.

This network of functions within a human association, this invisible order into which individual purposes are constantly being introduced, does not owe its origin simply to a summation of wills, a common decision by *many* individual people. It was not on the basis of a free decision by many, a *contrat social*, and still less on the basis of referenda or elections, that the complex and highly differentiated functional web of the present has emerged very gradually from the relatively simple early-medieval chains of functions that linked people together as priests, knights and bondsmen, for example, in the West. The people of the West did not come together at some time, as if from a state devoid of relationships, and, by a vote and the will of the majority, decide to distribute functions in accordance with the current scheme, as tradesmen, factory directors, policemen and workers. On the contrary, votes and elections, bloodless trials of strength between different functional groups, have become possible as permanent institutions of social control only in connection with a very specific structure of social functions. Underlying each such additive agreement is a pre-existing *functional* connection between these people which is not only summational. Its structure and tensions are directly or indirectly expressed in the result of the vote. And this functional structure can only be changed or developed within fairly narrow limits by majority decisions, votes and elections. The web of interdependent functions by which people are tied to each other has a weight and laws of its own which leave only a precisely circumscribed scope for bloodless compromises – and every majority decision is in the last analysis such a compromise.

But although this functional context has its own laws on which all the goals of individuals and all decisions counted in voting slips ultimately depend, although its structure is not the creation of particular individuals or even many individuals, no more is it something existing outside individuals. All these interdependent functions, those of the factory director or the fitter, of a married woman without a profession or of a friend or a father, are all functions which a person has for other people, an individual for other individuals. But each of these functions relates to others; it is dependent on their functions as they are on it. By virtue of this ineradicable interdependence of individual functions the actions of many separate individuals, particularly in a society as complex as our own, must incessantly link together to form long chains of actions if the actions of each individual are to fulfil their purposes. And in this way each individual person is really tied; he is tied by living in permanent functional dependence on other people; he is a link in the chains binding other people, just as all others, directly or indirectly, are links in the chains which bind him. These chains are not visible and tangible in the same way as iron chains. They are more elastic, more variable, more changeable; but they are no less real, and certainly no less strong. And it is this network of the functions which people have for each other, it and nothing else, that we call "society". It represents a special kind of sphere. Its structures are what we call "social structures". And if we talk of "social laws" or "social regularities", we are referring to nothing other than this: the autonomous laws of the relations between individual people.

To close the gulf that seems so often to open in thought between the individual and society is no simple task. It demands a peculiar effort of thought; for the difficulties we have to contend with in all reflections on the relation of individual to society stem – as far as they originate in *ratio* – from specific mental habits which at present are all too firmly rooted in the consciousness of each of us. Generally speaking, it seems at the present stage of thinking to be extraordinarily difficult for the majority of people to conceive that relationships can have a structure and a regularity of their own. Regularity, we are accustomed to think, is something proper to substances, objects or bodies that can be directly perceived by the senses. The pattern of a relationship, an inner voice tells us, must be explained by the structure and laws of the perceptible objects which´are related together in it. It seems self-evident to us that the only fruitful way of understanding composite units is to dissect them. Our thinking should start, so it seems to us, from the smaller units which make up the bigger ones through their relationships to each other. To investigate these as they are "in themselves", independently of all their relations to each other, seems the indispensable first step. The relations between them, and thus the large unit they form together, we involuntarily think of as something added later, a kind of after-thought.

But these mental habits, fruitful as they may be up to a point in dealing with experiences of inanimate substances, constantly give rise to specific anomalies when dealing in thought with the different kind of experiences we have of ourselves, of people and of society. These mental habits constantly force particular groups of people, whose ideas, in conjunction with their specific social experiences, focus above all on the *autonomy* of laws of human relationships, to conceal from themselves the fact that these are, all the same, laws of human *relationships*. Since they can only conceive regularities as the regularities of substances or of substantial forces, they unconsciously attribute to the regularities of human relationships which they observe a substance of their own beyond the individuals. On the basis of these specific social regularities, they can conceive of society only as something supra-individual. They invent as the medium supporting these regularities either a "collective mind" or a "collective organism" or, as the case may be, supra-individual mental and material "forces" by analogy with natural forces and substances. Opposed to them on the other side are groups whose ideas focus above all on the human individuals. They see quite clearly what is concealed to the others: that all that which we call "social structures and laws" is nothing other than the structures and laws of the relations between individual people. But like the first group they are incapable of imagining that relationships can themselves have structures and regularities of their own; like them they involuntarily think of these structures and regularities not as a peculiarity of relations *between* tangible units but as a peculiarity of such bodily units. But they, in keeping with their different social experiences and interests, believe the tangible substance of social structures and regularities to be located within the individual seen in isolation. If the former group, by virtue of their insight into the autonomous laws of human relations, unconsciously attribute a substance of its own to this regularity, the latter find it inconceivable that relations *between* individuals should have a structure and laws of their own; they involuntarily imagine that the explanation of the structures and laws of the relations between individuals is to be sought in the "nature" or "consciousness" of the individuals, as they are "in themselves" prior to all relationships, and in their own structure and regularities. It is from individuals, as the "atoms" and "smallest particles" of society, so it seems to them, that one's thinking should start, building up a concept of their relations to each other, of society, as something coming later. In a word, they conceive individuals as firm posts between which the line of relationships is strung afterwards. The others, with their eye fixed on the autonomy of human relationships, think of society as something existing before and independently of individuals; the latter group, with their different interests, think of individuals as something existing prior to and independently of society. And for one group as for the other certain areas of facts cannot be dealt with by thought. For one as for the other an unbridgeable mental gulf opens between social and individual phenomena.

The relationship between individuals and society is something unique. It has no analogue in any other sphere of existence. All the same, experience gained in observing the relation of part to whole in other spheres can to a certain extent help us here. It can help to loosen and extend the mental habits that have been referred to. One does not understand a melody by considering each of its notes in isolation, unrelated to the other notes. Its structure too is nothing other than the structure of the relations *between* different notes. It is similar with a house. What we call its structure is not the structure of the individual stones but of the relations *between* the individual stones of which it is built; it is the complex of functions the stones have in relation to each other within the unity of the house. These functions, and the structure of the house, cannot be explained by thinking about the shape of the individual stones independently of their relations to each other; on the contrary, the shape of the stones can only be explained in terms of their function within the whole functional complex, the structure of the house. One must start by thinking about the structure of the whole in order to understand the form of the individual parts. These and many other phenomena have one thing in common, different as they may be in all other respects: *to understand them it is necessary to give up thinking in terms of single, isolated substances and to start thinking in terms of relationships and functions.* And our thinking is only fully equipped to understand our social experience once we have made this switch.

Let us imagine as a symbol of society a group of dancers performing court dances, such as the *française* or *quadrille*, or a country round dance. The steps and bows, gestures and movements made by the individual dancer are all entirely meshed and synchronized with those of other dancers. If any of the dancing individuals were contemplated in isolation, the functions of his or her movements could not be understood. The way the individual behaves in this situation is determined by the relations of the dancers to each other. It is similar with the behaviour of individuals in general. Whether they meet as friends or enemies, parents or children, man and wife or knight and bondsman, king and subjects, manager and employees, however individuals behave is determined by past or present relations to other people. Even if they withdraw from all other people as hermits, gestures away from others no less than gestures towards them are gestures in relation to others. Of course, an individual can easily leave a dance if he wishes to, but people do not join up to form a society solely out of a desire for dance and play. What binds them to society is the fundamental disposition of their nature.

Indeed, no other image gives us an adequate impression of the importance which the relations between people have for the make-up of the individual. Nothing except an exploration of the nature and structure of these relations themselves can give an idea of how tightly and to what depth the interdependence of human functions binds the individual. Nothing else, in a word, gives a clearer image of the integration of individuals to form a society. But to gain greater clarity in this direction more than a mere revision of mental habits is needed. What is needed is a fundamental revision of the whole traditional make-up of self-consciousness.[1]

II

Half consciously, half unconsciously, most people carry about with them even today a peculiar myth of creation. They imagine that in the "beginning" a single person first appeared on earth and was then joined afterwards by other people. That is how the Bible describes it. But echoes of this form of consciousness show themselves in various other versions today. The old Adam makes a secularized reappearance in talk about the "primal man" or the "original father". It seems as if grown-up people, in thinking about their origins, involuntarily lose sight of the fact that they themselves and all adults came into the world as little children. Over and over again, in the scientific myths of origin no less than in the religious ones, they feel impelled to imagine: In the beginning was a single human being, who was an adult.

As long as we remain within the realm of experience, however, we are obliged to register that the single human being is engendered by and born of other human beings. Whatever the ancestors of humanity may have been, as far as we can see back into the past we see an unbroken chain of parents and children, who in turn become parents. And one cannot understand how and why individual people are bound together in a larger unity by and with each other if one conceals this perception from oneself. Each individual is born into a group of people who were there before him. Not only that: each individual is by nature so constituted that he needs other people who were there before him in order to be able to grow up. One of the basic conditions of human existence is the simultaneous presence of a number of interrelated people. And if, to symbolize one's own self-image, one needs a myth of origin, it seems time to revise the traditional myth: In the beginning, one might say, was not a single person, but several people who lived with each other, who caused each other joy and pain as we do, who came into being through each other and passed away into each other, as we do, a social unit large or small.

But there is no such leap out of nothingness, and no myth of origin is needed to make comprehensible the primal social relatedness of the individual, his natural dependence on a life with other people. The facts directly before us are enough.

At birth individual people may be very different through their natural constitutions. But it is only in society that the small child with its malleable and relatively undifferentiated mental functions is turned into a more complex being. Only in relation to other human beings does the wild, helpless creature which comes into the world become the psychologically developed person with the character of an individual and deserving the name of an adult human being. Cut off from such relations he grows at best into a semi-wild human animal. He may grow up bodily; in his psychological make-up he remains like a small child. Only if he grows up in a group does the small human being learn connected speech. Only in the society of other, older people does he gradually develop a specific kind of far-sightedness and instinct control. And which language he learns, which pattern of instinct control and adult make-up develops in him, depends on the structure of the group in which he grows up, and finally on his position in this group and the formative process it entails.

Even within the same group the relationships allotted to two people, their individual histories, are never quite the same. Each person advances from a unique position within his network of relationships through a unique history to his death. But the differences between the paths followed by different individuals, between the positions and functions through which they pass in the course of their lives, are fewer in simpler societies than in complex ones. And the degree of individualization of adults in the latter societies is accordingly greater. Paradoxical as it may seem at the present stage in the development of mental habits, the individuality and the social relatedness of a person are not only not antithetical to each other, but the special shaping and differentiation of mental functions that we refer to as "individuality" is only possible for a person who grows up in a group, a society.

Undoubtedly, people also differ in their natural constitutions. But the constitution a person brings with him into the world, and particularly the constitution of his or her psychical functions, is malleable. The new-born child is no more than a preliminary sketch of a person. His adult individuality does not grow necessarily and along a single path from what we perceive as his distinguishing features, his special constitution, as a plant of a particular species grows from its seed: the distinctive constitution of a new-born child allows scope for a great wealth of possible individualities. It shows no more than the limits and the position of the dispersion curve on which the individual form of the adult can lie. How this form actually develops, how the malleable features of the new-born child gradually harden into the adult's sharper contours, never depends solely on his constitution and always on the nature of the relations between him and other people.

These relationships, for example, between father, mother, child and siblings within a family, variable as they may be in details, are determined in their basic structure by the structure of the society into which the child is born and which existed *before* him. They are different in societies with different structures. For this reason the constitutional peculiarities with which a human being comes into the world have a very different significance for the relationships of the individual in different societies, and in different historical epochs of the same society. Similar natural constitutions in new-born babies lead to a very different development of consciousness and instincts, depending on the pre-existing structure of relationships in which they grow up. Which individuality a human being finally evolves depends not only on his or her natural constitution but on the whole process of individualization. Undoubtedly, the person's distinctive constitution has an ineradicable influence on his or her entire fate. A sensitive child can expect a different fate to a less sensitive one in the same family or society. But this fate, and thus the individual shape which an individual slowly takes on in growing up, is not laid down from the first in the inborn nature of the baby. What comes of its distinctive constitution depends on the structure of the society in which it grows up. Its fate, however it may turn out in detail, is as a whole society-specific. Accordingly, the more sharply delineated figure of the grown-up, the individuality that gradually emerges from the less differentiated form of the small child as it interacts with its fate, is also society-specific. In keeping with the changing structure of western society, a child of the twelfth century develops a different structure of instincts and consciousness from that of a twentieth-century child. It has emerged clearly enough from the study of the civilizing process to what extent the general modelling and thus the individual shaping of an individual person depends on the historical evolution of the social standard, on the structure of human relationships. Advances of individualization, as in the Renaissance, for example, are not the consequence of a sudden mutation within individual people or of the chance conception of a specially high number of gifted people; they are social events, consequences of a breaking up of old groupings or a change in the social position of the artist-craftsman, for example. In short, the consequences of a specific restructuring of human relationships.

From this side, too, it is easy to lose sight of the fundamental importance of the relations between people for the individual in their midst. And these difficulties too result, at least in part, from the type of thought-models that are used in thinking about these relationships. As so often, these models are derived from the simplest relationships between three-dimensional bodies. The effort of re-orientation needed to break free of these models is certainly no less than that which was necessary when physicists began thinking in terms of the relationships between bodies, rather than starting from individual bodies such as the sun or the moon. The relation between people is often imagined like that between billiards balls: they collide and roll apart. But the interaction between people, the "network phenomena" they produce are essentially different from the purely additive interactions of physical substances.

Think, for example, of a relatively simple form of human relationship, a conversation. One partner speaks, the other replies. The first responds and the second again replies. If one considers not only the individual remark and counter-remark but the course taken by the conversation as a whole, the sequence of interwoven ideas pushing each other along in continuous interdependence, one is dealing with a phenomenon that cannot be adequately represented either by the physical model of the action and reaction of balls, or by the physiological model of the relationship between stimulus and reaction. The ideas of either party may change in the course of the conversation. It may be, for example, that a certain agreement is arrived at by the partners in the course of the conversation. One might convince the other. Then something from one passes into the other. It is assimilated into his or her individual structure of ideas. It changes this structure, and is in its turn modified by being incorporated into a different system. The same applies if opposition arises in the conversation. Then the ideas of one party enter into the inner dialogue of the other as an adversary, and so drive on his thoughts. The special feature of this kind of process, that we might call a network-figure, is that in its course each of the partners forms ideas that were not there before, or pursues further ideas already present. But the direction and the order followed by this formation and transformation of ideas are not explained solely by the structure of one partner or the other but by the relation between the two. And precisely this fact that people change in relation to each other and through the relationship to each other, that they are continuously shaping and reshaping themselves in relation to each other, is characteristic of the phenomenon of the network in general.

Suppose someone tried to view the sequence of answers given by one of the partners in such a conversation as a separate unity existing with its own order independently of the network-figure of the conversation: that would be much as if one were to consider a person's individuality as something independent of the relations in which he finds himself, the constant weaving of threads through which he has become what he is. That people – unlike billiard balls – evolve and change in and through their relationships to each other may not be quite clear as long as one thinks exclusively of adults, whose characters, whose structures of consciousness and instinct have become more or less fixed. They too are certainly never quite complete and finished. They too can change within their context of relationships, if with some difficulty and usually only in their more conscious self-control. But what we have called a "network" here to denote the whole relationship of individual and society, can never be understood as long as "society" is imagined, as is so often the case, essentially as a society of individuals who were never children and who never die. One can only gain a clear understanding of the relation of individual and society if one includes in it the perpetual growing up of individuals within a society, if one includes the process of individualization in the theory of society. The historicity of each individual, the phenomenon of growing up to adulthood, is the key to an understanding of what "society" is. The sociality integral to a human being only becomes apparent if one is aware what relations to other people mean for a small child.

The child is not only malleable or adaptable to a far greater degree than adults. It *needs* to be adapted by others, it *needs* society in order to become physically adult. In the child it is not only ideas, not only conscious behaviour that is constantly formed and transformed in and through its relations to others, but its instinctual tendencies, its instinct-controlled behaviour. Of course, the instinct-figures which slowly evolve in the new-born child are never simply a copy of what is done to him by others. They are entirely his. They are *his* response to the way in which his instincts and emotions, which are by nature orientated towards other people, are responded to and satisfied by these others. Only on the basis of this continuous instinctual dialogue with other people do the elementary, unformed impulses of the small child take on a more definite direction, a clearer structure. Only on the basis of such an instinctual dialogue does there develop in the child the complex psychical self-control by which human beings differ from all other creatures: a more or less individual character. In order to become psychically adult, a human individual, the child cannot do without the relation to older and more powerful beings. Without the assimilation of pre-formed social models, of parts and products of these more powerful beings, without the shaping of his psychical functions which they bring about, the child remains, to repeat the point, little more than an animal. And just because the helpless child needs social modelling in order to become a more individualized and complex being, the individuality of the adult can only be understood in terms of the relationships allotted to him or her by fate, only in connection with the structure of the society in which he or she has grown up. However certain it may be that each person is a complete entity in himself, an individual who controls himself and can be controlled or regulated by no one else if he does not do so himself, it is no less certain that the whole structure of his self-control, both conscious and unconscious, is a network product formed in a continuous interplay of relationships to other people, and that the individual form of the adult is a society-specific form.

The new-born, the small child – no less than the old man – has a socially appointed place shaped by the specific structure of the particular human network. If his function for his parents is unimportant or, through a shift in the social structure, less important than before, people either have fewer children or, in some cases, kill those already born. There is no zero-point of the social relatedness of the individual, no "beginning" or sharp break when he steps into society as if from outside as a being untouched by the network and then begins to link up with other human beings. On the contrary, just as parents are needed to bring a child into the world, just as the mother feeds the child first with her blood and then with nourishment from her body, the individual always exists, on the most fundamental level, in relation to others, and this relation has a particular structure specific to his society. He takes on his individual stamp from the history of these relationships, these dependences, and so, in a broader context, from the history of the whole human network within which he grows up and lives. This history and this human network are present in him and are represented by him, whether he is actually in relationships to others or on his own, actively working in a big city or shipwrecked on an island a thousand miles from his society. Robinson Crusoe, too, bears the imprint of a particular society, a particular nation and class. Isolated from all relations to them as he is on his island, he behaves, wishes and plans by their standard, and thus exhibits different behaviour, wishes and plans to Friday, no matter how much the two adapt to each other by virtue of their new situation.

III

There is today a widespread modelling of the self-image which induces the individual to feel and think as follows: "I am here, entirely on my own; all the others are out there, outside me; and each of them goes his way, just like me, with an inner self which is his true self, his pure 'I', and an outward costume, his relations to other people." This attitude towards themselves and others appears to those who have adopted it as entirely natural and obvious. It is neither one nor the other. It is an expression of a peculiar historical moulding of the individual by the network of relations, by a form of communal life with a very specific structure. What speaks through it is the self-consciousness of people who have been compelled to adopt a very high degree of restraint, affect control, renunciation and transformation of instinct, and who are accustomed to relegating a large number of functions, instinct-expressions and wishes to private enclaves of secrecy withdrawn from the view of the "outside world", or even to the cellar of their own psyche, the semi-conscious or unconscious. In a word, this kind of self-consciousness corresponds to the psychological structure that is established at certain stages of a civilizing process.[2] It is characterized by an especially strong differentiation and tension between the social commands and prohibitions inculcated as self-restraint, and the uncontrolled or repressed instincts and inclinations within the human being himself. It is this conflict within the individual, the "privatization" or exclusion of certain spheres of life from social intercourse, their association with socially instilled fear in the form of shame and embarrassment, for example, which causes the individual to feel that "inside" himself he is something that exists quite alone, without relations to other people, and that only becomes related "afterwards" to others "outside". However genuine, however true this idea may be as an expression of the special structure of the consciousness and instincts of individuals at a certain stage of the movement of civilization, it is a very inadequate expression of the true relationship between human beings. The gulf and the intense conflict which the highly individualized people of our stage of civilization feel within themselves are projected by their consciousness into the world. In their theoretical reflection they appear as an existential gulf and an eternal conflict between individual and society.

What is more, the manner in which society brings about the adaptation of the individual to his adult functions very often accentuates the split and tension within his psyche. The more intensive and all-embracing the control of instincts, the more stable the super-ego formation required by the performance of adult functions in a society, the larger, inevitably, grows the distance between the behaviour of children and adults; the more difficult becomes the individual civilizing process and the longer the time needed to prepare children for adult functions. Just because the discrepancy between the attitude of children and that required of an adult is so great, the young person is no longer placed as a child on the lowest rung of the function-career he is destined to climb, as in simpler societies. He does not learn directly through serving an adult master of his future function, like the page of a knight or the apprentice of a guildmaster. He is first removed from the sphere of adults for a long and still growing period. Young people being prepared for a wider and wider range of functions are no longer trained directly but indirectly for adult life, in specialized institutes, schools and universities.

The tasks open to the mass of individuals in a society with so many tensions and such an advanced division of labour as ours require, for as long as work takes up the major part of the day, a fairly narrow specialization. They therefore allow only a rather narrow and one-sided scope for the faculties and inclinations of the individual. Moreover, the prospects of a widening of this scope at a stage of transition from a society with relatively open opportunities to one with relatively closed opportunities, diminish constantly. Between life in the reserves of youth and in the rather restricted and specialized field of adult work there is seldom a true continuity. Very often the transition from one to the other is a sharp break. Often enough the young person is given the widest possible horizon for his knowledge and wishes, a comprehensive view of life while growing up; he exists in a kind of blessed island for youth and dreams, which stands in curious contrast to the life awaiting him as an adult. He is encouraged to develop diverse faculties for which adult functions in the present structure allow no scope, and diverse inclinations which the adult has to suppress. This reinforces still further the inner tension and split within the individual's psyche that was referred to earlier. Not only the high degree of control and transformation of instinct but the limitations and specialization imposed by adult functions, the intensity of competition and the tensions between various adult groups, all this makes the conditioning of the individual especially difficult. The likelihood that it will be in some way unsuccessful, that the balance between personal inclinations and social tasks will be unattainable for the individual, becomes extremely great.

The advance of the division of functions and of civilization at certain stages is therefore increasingly accompanied by the feeling in individuals that in order to maintain their positions in the human network they must allow their true nature to wither. They feel constantly impelled by the social structure to violate their "inner truth". They feel unable to do what best suits their faculties, or to become what they really wanted to become. The pressure exerted on the individual by the human network, the restrictions its structure imposes on him and the tensions and splits all this produces in him, are so great that a thicket of unrealizable and unresolved inclinations grows up in the individual; these inclinations are seldom revealed to the eyes of others or even to the individual's own consciousness.[3]

A widely held conception of the relation of individual to society vividly expresses this stage of development. In this situation it often seems to the individual that his or her true self, his soul, is locked up in something alien and external called "society" as in a cell. He has the feeling that from the walls of this cell, from "outside", other people, alien powers are exerting their influence on his true self like evil spirits, or sometimes benign ones; they seem to be tossing light or heavy balls on to him, which leave behind in the self deeper or shallower impressions.

This is the vision underlying, for example, the widely disseminated "milieu theory" and appearing to validate the nebulous concept of the "environment". This is the attitude which is more or less easily discernible in most current reflections on the relation of individual and society. The argument between the different schools of thought really only concerns the question how deep and how essential to the shaping of the individual are the pressures and influences exerted by this "external" society. Some say they are of only slight importance, and that what primarily determines the shape of the individual are the individual's own inner laws, which are independent of his relations to others, his inborn "inner" nature. Others say the importance of this "inner" process is relatively slight and that the crucial shaping influence comes from "outside". Others again favour a kind of compromise; they imagine an interaction between "inside" and "outside", between "psychical" and "social" factors, though they tend to give one or the other greater emphasis.

The conception underlying all these ideas, the antithesis between the "pure self" – the subject of psychology – which enters relationships with other people as if from outside, and a society – the subject of sociology – which stands opposite the individual as something existing outside him, this conception undoubtedly has some value as an expression of a particular historical stage of the human network and the corresponding form of human self-consciousness. But it proves inadequate if the field of enquiry is widened, if the individual does not start directly from himself and his own feelings in reflecting on society, but sees himself and his self-consciousness in the larger context of historical evolution. One might ask how and why the structure of the human network and the structure of the individual both change at the same time in a certain manner, as in the transition from a warrior to a court society, or from this to a middle-class working society, when the wishes of individuals, their instinct and thought structure, even the *type of individualities*, are also changed. One finds then – in adopting a wider, dynamic viewpoint instead of a static one – that the vision of an irreducible wall between one human being and all others, between inner and outer worlds, evaporates to be replaced by a vision of an incessant and irreducible intertwining of individual beings, in which everything that gives their animal substance the quality of a human being, primarily their psychical self-control, their individual character, takes on its specific shape in and through relationships to others.

Our tools of thinking are not mobile enough adequately to grasp network phenomena, our words not yet supple enough to express this simple state of affairs simply. To get a closer view of this kind of interrelationship one might think of the object from which the concept of the network is derived, a woven net. In such a net there are many individual threads linked together. Yet neither the totality of the net, nor the form taken by each thread in it, can be understood in terms of a single thread alone or even all the threads considered singly; it is understood solely in terms of the way they are linked, their relationship to each other. This linking gives rise to a system of tensions to which each single thread contributes, each in a somewhat different manner according to its place and function in the totality of the net. The form of the individual thread changes if the tension and structure of the whole net change. Yet this net is nothing other than a linking of individual threads; and within the whole each thread still forms a unity in itself; it has a unique position and form within it.

This is no more than an image, rigid and inadequate like all images of this kind. But as a model for thinking about human networks it is sufficient to give a somewhat clearer idea of the manner in which a net of many units gives rise to an order which cannot be studied in the individual units. However, the relations between people can never be expressed in simple spatial forms. And it is a static model. It serves its purpose somewhat better if one imagines the net in constant movement as an incessant weaving and unweaving of connections. The individual actually grows in this way from a network of people existing before him into a network that he helps to form. The individual person is not a beginning and his relations to other people have no beginnings. Just as in a continuous conversation the questions of one evoke the answers of the other and vice versa, and just as a particular part of the conversation does not arise from one or the other alone but from the relation between the two, from which it is to be understood, so each gesture and act of the infant is neither the product of his "inside" nor of his "environment", nor of an interaction between an "inside" and an "outside" which were originally separate, but a function and precipitate of relations, and can be understood – like the figure of a thread in a net – only from the totality of the network. Likewise the speech of others develops in the growing child something which is entirely his own, entirely *his* language, and at the same time a product of his relations to others, an expression of the human network within which he lives. In the same way, ideas, convictions, affects, needs and character traits are produced in the individual through inter-course with others, things which make up his most personal "self" and in which is expressed, for this very reason, the network of relations from which he has emerged and into which he passes. And in this way this self, this personal "essence", is formed in a continuous interweaving of needs, a constant desire and fulfil-ment, an alternating taking and giving. It is the order of this incessant interweaving without a beginning that determines the nature and form of the individual human being. Even the nature and form of his solitude, even what he feels to be his "inner life",[4] is stamped by the history of his relationships – by the structure of the human network in which, as one of its nodal points, he develops and lives as an individual.

IV

We normally imagine the human being today as having a number of psychical compartments. We distinguish between "mind" and "soul", "reason" and "feeling", "consciousness" and "instinct" or "ego" and "id". But the sharp differentiation of psychical functions evoked by such words is not, to reiterate the point, something simply given by nature. It only occurs in a human being when he or she grows up as a child in a group, a society of people. It does not occur, like physical growth, for example, as a result of an inherited natural mechanism, but emerges from the interweaving of the "natures" of many people. And however sharply our concepts may express it, this differentiation only comes into being gradually, even in adults, with the increasing differentiation of the human societies themselves. It is a product of a socio-historical process, of a transformation in the structure of communal life.

Furthermore, the concepts with which we try to express this sharper differentiation of psychological functions in the adults of our society show a marked tendency to conceal the specifically *functional* character of what we call the "psyche" in a particular way. "Reason", "mind", "consciousness" or "ego", no matter how they may differ in detail, no matter how differently they draw the dividing line within the human psyche, all give the impression of substances rather than functions, of something at rest rather than in motion. They seem to refer to something which exists in the same way as the stomach or the skull. In reality they are quite specific functions of the human organism. They are functions which – unlike those of the stomach or the bones, for example – are *directed* constantly towards *other* people and things. They are particular *forms of a person's self-regulation in relation to other people and things*.

The same is true of the instincts and affects. Even in psychoanalytic literature one sometimes finds statements to the effect that the "id" or the instincts are unchanging *if one disregards changes in their direction*. But how is it possible to disregard this directedness in something as fundamentally *directed* at something else as human instincts? What we call "instincts" or the "unconscious" is also a particular form of self-regulation in relation to other people and things, though one which, given the sharp differentiation of psychical functions, no longer directly controls behaviour but does so by various detours.

In a word, within the totality of the human organism there are two different but entirely interdependent areas of functions. There are organs and functions that serve to maintain and constantly reproduce the organism itself, and there are organs and functions which serve the relations of the organism to other parts of the world and its self-regulation in such relations. We usually express the difference between these two areas of functions – in an over-static and substantializing way – by the distinction between "body" and "soul". What we refer to as "soul" or as pertaining to the "psyche" is in reality nothing but *the structure formed by these relation-functions*. The human being is not, as a particular historical form of human self-consciousness makes it appear, simply a closed container with various compartments and organs, a being which in its natural organization has, to begin with, nothing to do with other things and beings, but is organized by nature as a part of a larger world. He or she is, in a sense, a vector, which continuously directs valencies of the most diverse kinds towards other people and things, valencies which are temporarily saturated and ever anew unsaturated. He or she is so made up by nature as to be able, and obliged, to enter into relationships with other people and things. And what distinguishes this natural dependence of human beings on friendly or hostile relations from the corresponding dependence of animals, what actually gives this human self-regulation in relation to others the character of a *psychological* self-regulation – in contradistinction to the so-called instincts of animals – is nothing other than its greater flexibility, its greater capacity to adapt to changing kinds of relation, its special malleability and mobility.

This high degree of malleability and adaptability in human relation-functions is on one hand a precondition for the fact that the structure of relations between people is so much more variable than in the case of animals; in a word, it is the basis of the fundamental historicity of human society. On the other hand it is responsible for the fact that man is to a special degree a social being, dependent on the society of other people. In other animals self-regulation in relation to other creatures and things is restricted in advance by reflex mechanisms to fairly narrow paths. Even in those animals closest to man in the sequence of organisms, a certain relaxation in this respect can be observed, a somewhat greater adaptability to changing relations, a slight widening of the paths of their self-regulation. But only in man is the loosening and malleability of relation-functions so great that for the individual human being a period of years is needed for the moulding of self-regulation by other people, a social moulding, in order for it to take on a specifically human form. What man lacks in inherited predetermination in his dealings with other beings must be replaced by a social determination, a sociogenic shaping of the psychical functions.

That the form taken by the psychical functions of a person can never be deduced solely from his or her inherited constitution but only from the working up of this constitution in conjunction with other people, from the structure of the society in which the individual grows up, is therefore finally explained by a peculiarity of human nature itself, the fairly high degree of freedom of human self-regulation from the control of inherited reflex mechanisms. The existence of this freedom is well enough known, though we have only a dim understanding of its origins in natural history. Thanks to it the individual's management of relations is capable of, and needs, a far higher degree of social moulding than that of other animals. Thanks to this social mould-ing the structure of behaviour, the form of self-regulation in relation to others, is more diverse in man than in all the other animals; and thanks to it this self-regulation becomes, in a word, more "individual". From this direction too the discontinuity in thought between society and individual begins to close.

This is also a point from which it is possible easily to demolish the artificial fences we erect today in thought, dividing human beings up into various areas of control: the domains of, for example, the psychologists, the historians, the sociologists. The structures of the human psyche, the structures of human society and the structures of human history are indissolubly complemen-tary, and can only be studied in conjunction with each other. They do not exist and move in reality with the degree of isolation assumed by current research. They form, with other structures, the subject matter of the single human science.

But from this overall viewpoint – sketchy as the view must remain at present – we also gain a deeper understanding of the basic fact of the social existence of man to which we have referred so often: the fact that the network of people has an order and is subject to laws more powerful than and different from what the individuals making up this network themselves plan and want. It is the greater freedom of human relations from the control of inherited automatic mechanisms that really clears the way for the free play of social network mechanisms. It is only through the relative freedom of behaviour from determination by inherited mechanisms, the gradual, uneven transformation of the so-called "instinctive" into the so-called "psychical" self-regulation of the organism in relation to others, that the regularities or laws that come into being through the interweaving and interdependence of individuals take on their full force. Just because humans are less tightly bound to organically prescribed paths than other animals in shaping their relations to each other and the rest of the world, the interweaving of their activities gives rise to laws and structures of a special kind. For just this reason, automatic change mechanisms, historical transformations are set in motion in the network that neither have their origin in the inherited human reflex apparatus nor – taken as a whole, as they actually occur – have been desired or planned by individual people, yet which are anything but chaotic. For just this reason the irrevocable interweaving of the actions, needs, thoughts and impulses of many people give rise to structures and structural transformations in a specific order and direction, that are neither simply "animal" or "natural" nor "spiritual", neither "rational" nor "irrational", but *social*.

And in this peculiarity of the human psyche, its special malleability, its natural dependence on social moulding, lies the reason why one cannot take single individuals as one's starting point in order to understand the structure of their relationships to each other, the structure of society. On the contrary, one must start from the structure of the relations *between* individuals in order to understand the "psyche" of the individual person. If the single individual entered human society like Adam, as a ready-made grown-up in a strange world, then indeed it would take a miracle or a pre-stabilized harmony to explain why the parts and the whole, the psychological make-up of individuals and the structure of a society at a given time correspond to each other and change with each other. As the relatively undifferentiated relation-control of the new-born child only becomes differentiated and regulated by human means in relation to other humans, what then emerges as the "soul" of the individual adult is not something which is "in itself" alien to society and asocial, but something which is from its very foundation a function of the relation-unit of a higher power that we call "society". The whole manner in which the individual sees and manages himself in his relations to others depends on the structure of the association or associations of which he learns to say "we".

The simplest illustration of this apparently very complex state of affairs repeatedly proves to be the psychological function of speech. By nature each person normally brings with him into the world a speech apparatus that is capable of articulation and that he can himself control. In this respect too the human being is not only capable of being attuned to communicate with others of his kind, but by nature he needs attunement by other people, social attunement, in order to become a human being in the full sense of the word. In man the control of this form of relation by speech and its apparatus is not restricted by natural automatic mechanisms to such a narrow range of expressions as in the other animals. It is far less bound by inheritance. What is fixed by heredity, the range or pitch of voice, for example, merely provides the framework for an infinite variety of possible articulation. One might argue over *how far* these possibilities are *limited* by certain hereditary characteristics, by the history of the ancestral society. Only precise experiments could show, for example, whether the accent of a native of Africa still retained something of the intonation of his ancestors if he were brought up *from the first day of his life* without any further contact with people from his original society, in a society speaking an entirely different language, and if all his instinctual relationships, the central levers of moulding during early childhood, were relations to people of this other society, and allowed him normal fulfilment. But whether the limits of malleability are somewhat narrower or wider, the fundamental situation remains the same: what decides which language is gradually deposited in the individual's language apparatus is the society in which he or she grows up. And the personal speech habits, the more or less individual style of speaking the individual may have as an adult, is a differentiation within the medium of the language with which he has grown up. It is a function of his individual history within his society and its history. Hereditary features undoubtedly have some influence on the nature of this individual differentiation. But it is an influence of a similar kind to that exerted by the peculiarities of an unhewn stone, for example, its greater or lesser hardness, its type of grain, on the richly articulated sculpture which the sculptor carves from it. And it is not so different with the actual subject matter that language seeks to express, thinking and feeling. It is no different with the whole self-regulation of a person in relation to other beings and things, his "psyche".

Within the division of labour of the sciences, psychology is thus allocated a rather curious task. The individual child, as it is born, is the outcome of a fate which has both a natural and a social dimension, the history of its ancestors which is lost to view in the obscurity of past millennia. The compulsive way in which the organism of the new-born child controls the processes within him, the development and reducing of organs in accordance with a pattern imprinted within him as a legacy of past generations, and the relatively small influence exerted on *this* form of self-regulation by the current social situation – these are the factors which cause us to regard the self-formation of the individual as governed by "natural laws". Even the specific self-regulatory functions with which psychology concerns itself, including the relation-functions, are certainly governed to an extent by natural laws, though to a lesser degree than the self-regulation of the organism in the development of organs. Psychology is concerned precisely with those functions of self-regulation which are less strictly determined than the others by the ancestral history of a person, and are more determinable by the present structure of his society and his actual fate within it. Because these more malleable control functions are not only able to be moulded by present society but need to be so moulded if they are to evolve into the complex self-control mechanism of an adult person, psychology finds itself confronted by a correspondingly complex task. On one hand it has to investigate the natural structure and laws of all the human self-regulatory functions that are directed towards other beings and things, which play a part in a person's relations to them and, through their natural malleability, form the material to be moulded by these relations. On the other, it has to trace the process whereby these more malleable control functions, in conjunction with a particular social structure and co-existence with other people, are differentiated in such a way as to give rise to a particular individual form. Finally, it has to illuminate the general structure of this process of differentiation and moulding, and to explain in detail how the particular form of behaviour-control that has been consolidated into a "character", an individual psychological make-up within the individual on the basis of a particular set of relations, a specific social moulding, subsequently functions in living together with other people. The first part of these tasks leads directly to an investigation of the physiological and biological regularities of the organism, the other to the investigation of the socio-historical structures and regularities on which the direction and form of individual differentiation depend.[5] In a word, psychology forms the bridge between the natural sciences and the social sciences.

V

Human beings are part of a natural order and of a social order. The preceding reflections have shown how this double character is possible. The social order, although quite unlike a natural order such as the order of the organs within an individual body, owes its very existence to a peculiarity of human nature. This peculiarity is the special mobility and malleability by which human behaviour-control differs from that of animals. Thanks to these qualities, what is in the animal largely an inherited part of its nature, a fixed pattern of behaviour-control in relation to other beings and things, has to be produced in the individual human being in and through the society of other people. And thanks to these qualities, regularities and automatic processes come into play which we call "social" in contradistinction to organic, natural regularities. The relaxing of the natural reflex-apparatus governing human behaviour is itself the outcome of a long process of natural history. But thanks to it, processes and transformations take place in human communal life that are not pre-programmed in human nature; thanks to it, societies and individual people within them have a history which is not natural history. Within the general coherence of nature they form an autonomous continuum of a special kind.

There are societies – the Australian aborigines, for example – in which the basic structure of the relations between people hardly changes perceptibly over centuries. There are other forms of communal life which contain a peculiar urge to transcend themselves in their mode of communal living without any extra-social causes needing to be involved. They are *directed* towards other forms of interpersonal relationships and institutions, whether or not these forms are actually attained. They are in the narrower sense of the word *historical*.

At the basis of these automatic mechanisms and tendencies of social change are particular forms of human relations, tensions between people of a specific kind and intensity. These tensions begin to be produced, to state the matter very generally, at a particular stage in the division of functions, when certain people or groups acquire a hereditary monopoly of the goods and social values on which other people depend, either for their livelihood or to protect or fulfil their social existence.

Among the goods that can be monopolized in this way, those serving to satisfy elementary needs such as hunger undoubtedly have special importance. But the monopolization of goods of this kind is only *one* kind of monopoly among others. Moreover, it never exists in isolation. Every "economic" monopoly of no matter what kind is directly or indirectly linked to another without which it cannot exist, with a monopoly of physical force and its instruments. This monopoly can take the form, as in feudal times, of an unorganized and decentralized monopoly of arms operated by large numbers of people or, as in the age of absolutism, of a monopoly of physical violence controlled by one individual. What we refer to as the "economic" sphere of interconnections – that sphere which is often regarded today, generalizing from the structure of the first phase of industrialization, as a separate sphere of history and the only driving force in it, the motor that sets all the other spheres in motion as a "superstructure" – itself depends on the monopoly of violence. It only becomes possible with the increasing differentiation of society, the formation of more stable centres of physical violence and internal pacification, allowing the emergence of the economy as a separate sphere within the wide fabric of human actions.

An economic sphere of interconnections does not come into being *solely*, as is sometimes assumed, because human beings have to satisfy their need to eat. Animals, too, are driven by hunger; but they do not engage in *economic* activity. Where they seem to do so it happens, as far as we can see today, on the basis of a more or less automatic, innate or "instinctive" predisposition of their self-regulation paths. Economic networks in the human sense only arise because human self-regulation in relation to other things and beings is *not* automatically restricted to the same degree to relatively narrow channels. One of the preconditions of an economy in the human sense is the peculiarly *psychological* character of human behaviour control. For any form of such economic activity to arise it is essential that super-ego or foresight functions intervene to regulate the elemental instinct functions of the individual, whether they be the desire for food, protection or whatever else. Only such intervention makes it possible for people to live together in a more or less regulated manner, for them to work together to a common pattern in procuring food, and for their communal life to give rise to various interdependent social functions. In a word, specifically social regularities – and therefore economic ones – only come into being through the peculiarity of human nature which distinguishes humans from all other creatures. For this reason all attempts to explain these social regularities from biological regularities or their patterns, all endeavours to make social science into a kind of biology or a part of the other natural sciences, are futile.

Human beings create a special cosmos of their own within the natural cosmos, and they do so by virtue of a relaxation of automatic natural mechanisms in managing their communal life. They form together a socio-historical continuum into which each individual person grows – as a part – from a particular point. What shapes and binds the individual within this human cosmos, and what gives him the whole scope of his life, is not the reflexes of his animal nature but the ineradicable connection between his desires and behaviour and those of other people, of the living, the dead and even, in a certain sense, the unborn – in a word, his dependence on others and the dependence of others on him, the functions of others for him and his function for others. This dependence is never due *solely* to his instincts on one hand or what is called thought, foresight, ego or super-ego, depending on the viewpoint of the observer, on the other, but is always a functional relationship based on both. In the same way, the specific tensions between different groups which generate an urge towards structural changes within this human continuum, which make it into a *historical* continuum, have two layers. In them, and even in their genesis, though to varying degrees, both short-term emotional and long-term super-ego impulses are always involved. These tensions would never arise without such elemental driving forces as hunger; but nor would they arise without longer-range impulses such as those expressed in the desire for property or for more property, for lasting security or for an elevated social position with power and superiority over others. Precisely the monopolization of the goods and values that satisfy such manifold instinctual demands, such sublimated forms of desire – that satisfy, in a word, the hunger of the ego and the super-ego – precisely this monopoly, together with the monopoly of that which satisfies basic hunger, is all the more important to the genesis of social tensions the further the differentiation of social functions, and therefore of psychical functions, advances, the more the normal standard of living of a society rises above the satisfaction of the most elementary nutritional and sexual needs.

Of course, the basic situation remains simple enough, no matter how complex the structure of social functions and thus the tensions between various functional groups may become. Even in the simplest societies known to us there is some form of division of functions between people. The further this division has advanced within a society and the more give and take there is between people, the more tightly are they bound together by the fact that one can only sustain his life and his social existence in conjunction with many others. At some stages the instruments of violence available to some may allow them to deny others what they need to secure and fulfil their social existence, or constantly to threaten, subjugate and exploit them; or the goals of some may actually require the social and physical existence of others to be destroyed. This brings into being within the network of interdependent people, function-groups and nations, tensions which may differ widely in nature and strength but which always have a very clear structure that can be precisely described. And it is tensions of this kind that, when they attain a certain strength and structure, generate an urge towards structural changes in society. Thanks to them the forms of relations and institutions within the society do not reproduce themselves in approximately the same form from generation to generation. Thanks to them certain forms of communal life tend constantly to move in a particular direction towards specific transformations without any external driving forces being involved.

Network forces of this kind are at the root, for example, of the

increasing division of functions which is of such decisive importance for the course of western history, leading at one stage to the
use of money, at another to the development of machines and
thus to the increased productivity of work and to a raising of the
living standard of more and more people. We find such automatisms in the manner in which, in the West, free craftsmen emerge
to confront the landowning class as the division of functions
advances; and in the subsequent emergence, over centuries in
which there was a very gradual shift in the balance of forces, of
noble and burgher groups, followed by capital-owning and
capital-less groups, as the poles of the most powerful tensions –
tensions which were certainly never planned or created by individual people. It is network forces of this kind that have in the
course of western history changed the form and quality of human
behaviour and the whole psychical regulation of behaviour,
pushing it in the direction of civilization. We see it in our own
time in the rigorous way in which the tensions that emerge in the
form of free competition within the human network tend towards
a narrowing of the sphere of competition and finally to the
formation of centralized monopolies. In this way, through network forces, peaceful periods of history have been produced and
are produced no less than turbulent and revolutionary ones,
flowering no less than ruin, phases of high art and of pale
imitation. All these changes have their origin not in the nature of
individual people but in the structure of the communal life of
many. History is always the history of a society, but, to be sure, of
a society of individuals.

Only from such a general perspective can it be fully understood
how changes of this kind – for example, the process of the
increasing division of labour or that of civilization – can follow a
very definite direction and order over many generations without
their actual course being planned or systematically executed by
individual people. And only from such a viewpoint can we finally
understand how such a change in human beings is possible
without some motor of change *outside* human beings. Our thinking today is still extensively governed by ideas of causality which

are inadequate to the process under discussion: we are strongly inclined to explain any change in a particular formation by a cause *outside* that formation. The mystery of the specifically socio-historical transformation only begins to be dispelled if one understands the following: that such changes need be caused neither by changes in nature outside human beings nor by changes in a "spirit" within individuals or nations. No evidence available to us indicates that during the centuries of the advance of western civilization any changes of a similar scale took place in the natural constellation, for example, the climate, or within the organic nature of man himself. The "environment" which changed – to use this often misused expression – was only the environment which people form for each other. During those centuries the sky stayed more or less the same, as did the organic nature of man and the geological structure of the earth. The only thing that changed and moved in a specific direction was the form of communal life, the structure of western society and with it the social influence on the individual and the form of his or her psychical functions.

It might be misleading to say that this continuum of human society is a "perpetual motion machine". Undoubtedly, this continuum constantly draws physical energy from the surrounding world. From the physical standpoint society is only a part of the mightier natural cosmos which as a whole is indeed a perpetual motion machine. But like the Gulf Stream within the ocean, for example, the continuum of interdependent human beings has a movement of its own within this mightier cosmos, a regularity and a tempo of change that are in their turn mightier than the will and plans of a single person within it.

VI

But once one has gained a clearer view of those aspects of social life which stand out more sharply from the historical flow when seen from above and over long stretches, one must revert to the other perspective, that one has from within the flow. Each of these perspectives, when isolated from the other, has its specific dangers. Each of them – the view of the airman and of the swimmer – shows the picture with a certain foreshortening. Each of them makes us inclined to give a one-sided emphasis. Only the two together give a more balanced picture.

Only by means of a certain detachment, by setting aside immediate wishes and personal sympathies, can one gain an undistorted view of the order of historical change, of the peculiar necessity with which the human network, having reached a certain pitch of tensions, is urged to move beyond itself, whether towards more comprehensive integration or towards relative disintegration, a victory of centrifugal forces. And the insight that one gains through such conscious detachment certainly loses none of its value if one then begins to look again through the eyes of someone who has to take decisions here and now within the historical flow. Only the longer-sighted perspective gives a certain security to the decisions taken under the pressure of short-term impulses. But it in turn needs to be balanced and complemented by that which is perceived better and more easily in the moment of action itself. If what strikes us most of all from the elevated viewpoint is the rigorous way in which the historical flow is constantly urged on in a particular direction, the person engaged in action within the flow is much more aware of how varied – often if not always – are the paths by which structures and tensions of one kind are able to turn themselves into structures of a different kind. To him, history seems like one of those mighty rivers which, although they always follow a particular direction, towards the sea, do not have a fixed, pre-ordained bed before them but a broad terrain within which they have to seek a definite course; within which, in other words, they can still form a bed in a large number of possible ways.

Undoubtedly, we are in general only in a position to gain a clear insight into the automatisms of historical change when we have not only the immediate present before us but the long history from which our time has emerged. A person who has to act and take decisions within the weft of his time is more likely to perceive another characteristic of the network which is no less important: its extraordinary elasticity. To express what the observer who has attained a certain detachment is struck by in the course of history, one has little choice at the present stage of thought and speech than to borrow words and images from the realm of inanimate nature. This is why terms such as "mechanism" and "automatism" have been used quite often here. But history is not, of course, a system of lifeless mechanical levers and automatisms of iron and steel, but a system of pressures exerted by living people on living people. Only when a special terminology has been developed for this system with its own special laws will it be possible to show with proper clarity how far these social "automatisms" differ from those of the machine shop. And while the observer overflying long stretches of history may notice first how little power individual people have over the main line of historical movement and change, the person acting within the flow may have a better chance to see how much can depend on individual people in individual situations, despite the fixed general direction. Only both observations together – far from contradicting each other – yield, if properly linked, a more revealing, more adequate picture.

One need only consider the effect of the competitive mechanism. If freely competing people or groups find themselves in violent conflict, they work, whether they want to or not, with certainty towards a reduction of the sphere of competition and towards a monopoly situation, no matter how often the process may be temporarily reversed, for example, by alliances of the weaker parties. To this extent the actions of the competitors are no more than levers in a social automatism. But which of the rivals is victorious, which of them is able to seize control of the opportunities of the others and so to administer the law of the competition mechanism, i.e. the decision which matters most to those involved, this decision is far less determined by the overall structure of the society involved than is the social mechanism itself. The outcome may depend very largely on the instinctual endowments, the personal energy and intelligence of one or more individuals within the rival groups. And the same applies to many other tensions the resolution of which prepares the ground for, or actually brings about, structural changes within a society. The axis along which tensions of a particular kind act, the direction in which they point beyond themselves, and the general structure towards which they are tending, are clearly delineated, whether the direction is towards "downfall", a disintegration of the existing structures and functions, or towards further integration along different axes of tension. But the forms and paths taken by these conflicts and transformations, and the speed with which they occur, are certainly not as strictly pre-ordained as the main line along which the social continuum moves, along which its axes of tension strain beyond themselves.

Every large and complex society has, in fact, both qualities: it is very firm and very elastic. Within it scope for individual decision constantly appears. Opportunities present themselves that can be either seized or missed. Crossroads appear at which people must choose, and on their choices, depending on their social position, may depend either their immediate personal fate or that of a whole family, or, in certain situations, of entire nations or groups within them. It may depend on their choices whether the complete resolution of the present tensions takes place in this generation or only in the next. It may depend on them which of the contending persons or groups within a particular system of tensions becomes the executor of the transformations towards which the tensions are straining, and on which side, in which place, the centres of the new forms of integration, towards which the older ones are moving by virtue of their tensions, will be located. But the opportunities between which a person has to choose in this manner are not themselves created by that person. They are prescribed and limited by the specific structure of his society and the nature of the functions the people exercise within it. And whichever opportunity he seizes, his deed becomes interwoven with those of others; it unleashes further chains of actions, the direction and provisional outcome of which depend not on him but on the distribution of power and the structure of tensions within this whole mobile human network.

No individual person, no matter how great his stature, how powerful his will, how penetrating his intelligence, can breach the autonomous laws of the human network from which his actions arise and into which they are directed. No personality, however strong, can, as the emperor of a purely agrarian feudal domain – to give an example at random – more than temporarily arrest the centrifugal tendencies the strength of which corresponds to the size of the territory. He cannot turn his society at one stroke into an absolutist or an industrial one. He cannot by an act of will bring about the more complex division of labour, the kind of army, the monetarization and the total transformation of property relations that are needed if lasting central institutions are to evolve. He is tied to the laws of the tensions between bondsmen and feudal lords on one hand and between competing feudal lords and the central ruler on the other.

One comes across very similar compulsions – if we look for related structures in more recent history – in, for example, the development of the United States of America. There, too, a particularly large area of territory was involved. There, too, we find on one hand slowly increasing tendencies towards centralization and on the other especially strong forces opposing greater centralization. As earlier in the immense territory of the medieval German empire, throughout the history of the United States, even though there was a far higher level of division of labour, the tensions between the centrifugal and the centripetal interests were extraordinarily strong. The continual struggles of individual states with the central authorities of the union, the long-successful resistance of the many banks and private monopolies to the stabilization of a central federal bank, the occasional occupation of the central positions by the centrifugal interests themselves, the difficulties in the way of uniform fiscal legislation, the struggle between silver and gold and the countless crises connected with these tensions, all that is sufficiently well known.

Was it a special incompetence which prevented the American statesmen for a long period from establishing publicly controlled central institutions as strong and stable as those in Europe? Anyone who finds himself in the midst of such networks, anyone who studies the history of the United States in detail, knows better. No matter who was raised to the central position in the United States by the various selection mechanisms, that person was irresistibly enmeshed in tensions of a kind and intensity with which European statesmen no longer had to contend, as a result of the longer integration and the relatively small size of the individual European territories.

Of course, the strength of the tensions *within* the territory of the United States was and is amply outweighed by the strength of the tensions *between* the different states of Europe. Whether the different poles of the axes of tension were represented by major figures as in the time of Jefferson and Hamilton, or by people of lesser stature, it was again and again the strength of these tensions within their society that laid down the actions to be taken by the American statesmen. And it was also due to the special strength of centrifugal interests, not to any special incompetence of the leading American statesmen, that the centre of gravity shifted much more slowly than in Europe towards the centripetal interests as the division of functions progressed. No personality, however great, could breach the law of this mighty human network. Within it the individual statesman, depending on his stature, had only a greater or lesser scope for decision.

But even if scope for individual decision emerges here as everywhere within the social network, there is no general formula which indicates how great this individual scope is for all phases of history and all types of societies. Precisely this is characteristic of the place of the individual within his society, that the nature and extent of the scope for decision open to him depend on the structure and the historical constellation of the society in which he lives and acts. In no type of society is there a complete absence of such scope. Even the social function of a slave leaves some room for individual decisions, narrow as it may be. And conversely, the possibility for a king or general to influence his own fate and that of others through his personal qualities is generally incomparably greater than for the socially weaker individuals of his society. The scope of the decisions taken by the representatives of such leading functions becomes immense in certain historical situations. And for them the form and extent of the individual scope for decision can vary considerably, according to the personal suitability and stature of the function's incumbent. Here the scope for decision is not only greater, it is more elastic; but it is never unlimited. And in the exercise of such leading functions, exactly as in the case of an ordinary slave, the range of the decisions and the extent of their scope are determined by the particular kind of integration which has given rise to these functions and continues for a period to reproduce them. The individual person is always bound to others in a very specific way through interdependence. But in different societies and in different phases and positions within the same society, the individual scope for decision differs in both kind and size. And what we call "power" is really nothing other than a somewhat rigid and undifferentiated expression for the special extent of the individual scope for action associated with certain social positions, an expression for an especially large social opportunity to influence the self-regulation and the fate of other people.

If, for example, the social power of people or groups in the same social area is exceptionally unequal, if socially weak and low-ranking groups without significant opportunities to improve their positions are coupled to others with monopoly control of far greater opportunities of social power, the members of the weak group have exceptionally little scope for individual decision. In this case any outstanding gifts or strongly individualized characteristics among the members of the weak group cannot be developed, or only in directions regarded as asocial from the standpoint of the existing social structure. Thus, for members of socially weak peasant classes living on the verge of hunger, for example, the only way to improve their lot is often to leave their land and take up the life of brigands. The leading position in such groups, the position of "robber chief", is here the only opportunity for taking a significant personal initiative. Within the framework of the normal social existence of such poor and deprived classes there is minimal scope for personal initiative. And it is quite certain that the social position and the fate of such a group, given the enormous discrepancy in the distribution of the instruments of social power, could be altered solely by the special stature and energy of one of its members who became its leader.

If groups with less divergent or more or less equal power within a society form the main poles of the axes of tension, the situation is different. In that case it may well depend on the determination and stature of a few people whether the centre of gravity shifts decisively to one side or the other at an opportune moment. In such a network constellation the scope for decision open to the persons holding the leading functions can be very large. But whether the individual's scope for decision is larger or smaller, whatever he decides allies him to some and alienates him from others. In large matters as in small he is bound to the distribution of power, the structure of dependence and tensions within his group. The possible courses he decides between are pre-ordained by the structure of his sphere of activity and its mesh. And, depending on his decision, the autonomous weight of this mesh works either for or against him.

We often hear it debated today whether history is made by individual great men or whether all people are interchangeable, a person's individuality counting for nothing in the march of history. But the discussion between these two poles takes place in a vacuum. It lacks the element which provides a basis for all discussion of human beings and their ways: continuous contact with experience. Given a choice of this kind there is no simple "yes" or "no". Even for the people we are accustomed to regarding as the greatest personalities in history, other people and their products, their acts, their ideas and their language were the medium within which they acted and on which they acted. The specific nature of their co-existence with other people allowed their activity, like that of everyone else, a certain scope and certain limits. A person's influence on others, his importance to them, may be especially large, but the autonomy of the network in which he acts is incomparably more powerful than he. Belief in the unlimited power of individual people over the course of history is wishful thinking.

No less unrealistic, however, is the opposite belief, that all people are of equal importance for the course of history, that people are interchangeable, the individual being no more than the passive vehicle of a social machine. The most elementary observation teaches us that the importance of different individuals for the course of historical events differs, that in certain situations and for the occupants of certain social positions individual character and personal decision can have considerable influence on historical events. Individual scope for decision is always limited, but it is also very variable in nature and extent, depending on the instruments of powers which a person controls. A glance at the nature of human integration is enough to make this variability of individual limits comprehensible. What bends and limits individuals, seen from the other side, is the exact opposite of this limitation: their individual activity, their ability to take decisions in very diverse and individual ways. The individual activity of some is the social limitation of others. And it depends only on the power of the interdependent functions concerned, the degree of reciprocal dependence, who is more able to limit whom by his activity.

We have referred several times to the curious party game that certain groups in western society are apt to indulge in over and over again. There are two opposed parties: one says, "Everything depends on the individual", the other, "Everything depends on society". The first group says: "But it is always particular individuals who decide to do this and not that." The others reply: "But their decisions are socially conditioned." The first group says: "But what you call 'social conditioning' only comes about because others want to do something and do it." The others reply: "But what these others want to do and do is also socially conditioned."

The spell which binds us to think in terms of such alternatives is beginning to break. For indeed, the way in which a person decides and acts has been developed in relationships to other people, in a modifying of his nature by society. But what is shaped in this way is not something merely passive, not a lifeless coin stamped like a thousand identical coins, but the active centre of the individual, the personal direction of his instincts and will; in a word, his real self. What is shaped by society also shapes in its turn: it is the self-regulation of the individual in relation to others which sets limits to their self-regulation. To put it in a nutshell, the individual is both coin and die at the same time. One person may have more of the die-function than another, but he is always a coin as well. Even the weakest member of society has his share in stamping and limiting other members, however small. The party game can only carry on *ad infinitum* because it separates like two *substances* what are in fact two inseparable *functions* of human beings as they live together.

For the two parties have a characteristic idea in common, and this identical basis shows the antagonists to be children of the same time. The whole debate tacitly assumes – as a point of secret collusion, the undiscussed basis of the discussion – that the "social" is what is "the same" or "typical" among a number of people, while what makes a person unique and different from all others – in short, a more or less pronounced individuality – is an extra-social element that is forthwith assigned, for rather obscure reasons, either a biological or a metaphysical origin according to taste. At this point thought and observation come to an end.

We have already stressed that this notion of individuality as the expression of an extra-social, natural core within the individual around which the "typical" or "social" features are accreted like a shell, is itself connected to a specific, historically determined inner life. This notion is connected to the tension between the ego and super-ego functions on one hand and the instinct functions on the other, a tension never entirely lacking in any society but especially strong and pervasive when the civilizing process has reached an advanced stage. This tension, the contradictions between the desires of the individual partly controlled by the unconscious, and the social demands represented by his super-ego, is what constantly nourishes the idea of the natural individual core in the shell conditioned by society or milieu. These contradictions make it appear self-evident to the individual that he is something separate "inside" while "society" and other people are "external" and "alien". This specific form of super-ego, this especially strong and semi-automatic restraint of all drives and affects directed at others, is what has allowed the individual – more and more perceptibly since the Renaissance – to perceive himself as the "subject" and the world as something separated from him by an abyss, the "object". It allows him to see himself as an observer outside the rest of nature, while nature confronts him as "landscape"; to feel himself to be an individual independent of all other people, and other people as an "alien" realm that originally had nothing to do with his "inner" being, an "environment", a "milieu", a "society". Only when the individual stops taking himself as the starting point of his thought, stops viewing the world like someone who looks from the "interior" of his house on to the street "outside", at the houses "opposite", and is able – by a new Copernican revolution of his thought and feeling – to see himself and his shell as part of the street, to see them in relation to the whole mobile human network, only then will his feeling gradually fade that he is something isolated and self-contained "inside" while the others are something separated from him by an abyss, a "landscape", an "environment", a "society".

But this heavy restriction on the emotions does not stand alone. Closely linked to this peculiarity of our inner lives are many others which contribute equally to making contrasting ideas like "inside" and "outside", "innate" and "socially conditioned", appear, with regard to ourselves, as eternal opposites, fundamental items in the arsenal of thought and consciousness. To give just a few examples, there is the special satisfaction associated for the individual, at the present stage of the development of self-consciousness, with the idea that he owes everything he regards as unique and essential in himself, to himself alone, to his "nature", and to no one else. The idea that "alien" people may play an integral part in the formation of one's own individuality seems today almost like an infringement of one's rights over oneself. Only that part of himself which a person can explain by his "nature" seems entirely his own. In explaining it by his nature, he involuntarily accredits it to himself as a positive achievement; and conversely, he tends to attribute anything in himself which he regards as a positive achievement to his inborn nature. To imagine that his special individuality, his "essence", is not a unique creation of nature, issuing from its womb suddenly and inexplicably as Athene sprang from the head of Zeus, to attribute one's own psychical gifts or even one's problems to something as fortuitous as one's relations to other people, something as transitory as human society, seems to the individual a devaluation which deprives his existence of meaning. The idea that one's individuality has emerged from imperishable nature, like the idea that it was created by God, seems to give a far more secure justification to all that which a person believes unique and essential to himself. It anchors individual qualities in something eternal and regular; it helps the individual to understand the necessity of being what he is. It explains to him with one word – the word "nature" – what is otherwise inexplicable in himself.

In this way, as a result of a peculiar disposition of our feelings and wishes, we constantly lose conscious sight of the fact that the "nature" of the psychical functions of human beings is not quite the same thing as the "nature" of the other functions which enable a body to maintain itself in a particular form. A radical revision of the prevailing consciousness will be needed before the veil of wishes and values which obscures our view in this direction can be lifted. What we call a person's "individuality" is, first of all, a peculiarity of his or her *psychical* functions, a structural quality of his or her self-regulation in relation to other persons and things. "Individuality" is an expression for the special way in which, and the special degree to which, the structural quality of one person's psychical control differs from another's. But this specific difference in people's psychical structures would not be possible if their self-regulation in relation to other people and things were determined by inherited structures in the same way and to the same degree as the self-regulation of the human organism, for example, in the reproduction of organs and limbs. The "individualization" of people is only possible because the former control is more malleable than the latter. And because of this greater malleability, words such as "nature" or "disposition" and all the related terms have a different meaning when applied to the psychical functions of people than when applied to the functions of organ reproduction or growth. In the latter case, superficially considered, the traditional idea of nature as a realm that does not change, or at least changes at a very slow pace, has some validity. But in the case of psychical functions, in their adaptation and interweaving in social life, we are dealing with natural entities that allow a much faster tempo of change, which embody an order of their own. To explore these functions and the way they are shaped by each other we need to develop special concepts.

At present the traditional terms are all too frequently used, without distinguishing whether they refer to psychical functions or the formation of organs and limbs. Experience with the bodily functions sets the tone. Concepts that have proved more or less fruitful in elucidating them continue to be used without any further basis, and often enough as models for exploring the human psyche. One thinks, feels and to an extent wishes that the individuality of a person, the distinctive structure of his or her self-regulation in relation to other people and things, exists in the same independent way, isolated from all relations, as one feels one's own body to exist in space. From this side too an idea is generated that the individual human being, with all the psychical qualities that distinguish him from other people, represents a self-contained cosmos, a nature apart, which originally had nothing to do with the rest of nature or other human beings. And by using models derived from physical functions in trying to understand psychical ones, we are constantly forced to think in terms of stereotyped opposites such as "inside" and "outside", "individual" and "society", "nature" and "milieu". The only choice left open to the individual seems to be whether to concede the decisive role in shaping a human being to one side or the other. The most that can be imagined is a compromise: "A little comes from outside and a little from inside; we only need to know what, and how much."

Psychical functions do not fit into this pattern. The natural dependence of a person on others, the natural orientation of psychical functions to relationships, and their adaptability and mobility within relationships, are phenomena that cannot be grasped by models based on substances or by spatial concepts such as "inside" or "outside". To understand them different conceptual means and a different basic vision are needed.

We have here attempted to take a few steps towards such means. The configuration of a person's psychical self-regulation – for example, his or her mother tongue – is, through that person's having grown up in a particular society, thoroughly "typical", and is *at the same time*, through his or her having grown up as a unique reference-point within the network of a society, thoroughly individual, i.e. it is a unique manifestation of this typical product. Individual animals are also different from each other "by nature", as, certainly, are individual people. But this inherited biological difference is not the same as the difference in the structure of psychical self-regulation in adults that we express by the term "individuality". To repeat the point, a person who grows up outside human society does not attain such "individuality" any more than an animal. Only through a long and difficult shaping of his or her malleable psychical functions in intercourse with other people does a person's behaviour-control attain the unique configuration characteristic of a specific human individuality. It is only through a social moulding process within the framework of particular social characteristics that a person evolves the characteristics and modes of behaviour that distinguish him or her from all the other members of his or her society. *Society not only produces the similar and typical, but also the individual.* The varying degree of individuation among the members of different groups and strata shows this clearly enough. The more differentiated the functional structure of a society or a class within it, the more sharply the psychical configurations of the individual people who grow up within it diverge. But however different the degree of this individuation may be, there is certainly no such thing as a zero-point of individuation among people who grow up and live within society. To a greater or lesser degree, the people of all the societies known to us are individual and different from each other down to the last detail of their configuration and behaviour, and society-specific, i.e. shaped and bound in the nature of their psychical self-regulation by a particular network of functions, a particular form of communal life which also shapes and binds all its other members. What are often conceptually separated as two different substances or two different strata within the human being, his "individuality" and his "social conditioning", are in fact nothing other than two different functions of people in their relations to each other, one of which cannot exist without the other. They are terms for the specific activity of the individual in relation to his fellows, and for his capacity to be influenced and shaped by their activity; for the dependence of others on him and his dependence on others; expressions for his function as both *die* and *coin*.

VII

If human beings were not by nature so much more malleable and mobile than animals in their behaviour-control, they would neither form an autonomous historical continuum together (a society), nor possess an individuality of their own. Animal societies have no history other than their "natural history"; and the individual animals within such a society do not differ from each other in their behaviour, are not individualizable, to the same extent as individual human beings.

But as human beings are attunable to each other to this extent, and as they also need such adaptation, the network of their relationships, their society, cannot be understood in terms of single individuals, as if each of them first of all formed a natural, self-contained cosmos. On the contrary, the individual can only be understood in terms of his communal life with others. The structure and configuration of an individual's behaviour-control depend on the structure of the relations between individuals. The root of all misunderstandings on the relation of individual and society lies in the fact that while society, the relations between people, has a structure and regularity of a special kind that cannot be understood in terms of the single individual, it does not possess a body, a "substance" outside individuals.

Such ideas may be easy or difficult to grasp, but the facts they refer to are simple enough: the individual person is only able to say "I" if and because he can at the same time say "we". Even the thought "I am", and still more the thought "I think", presupposes the existence of other people and a communal life with them – in short, a group, a society. Of course, theoretical reflection alone is not enough, and a different structure of individual self-consciousness, a different self-justification of the individual would be needed to explore all the ramifications of this state of affairs. Only by a change in the structure of interpersonal relationships, a different structure of individualities, could a better harmony be established between social pressures and demands on one hand and individual needs, the desire of people for justification, meaning, fulfilment, on the other. Only then could a person's knowledge that everything he is and becomes is so in relation to other people, develop from a theoretical insight into a guideline for action and behaviour. Here it must be enough to create a terminology for the simple state of affairs itself. Society with its regularity is nothing outside individuals; nor is it simply an "object" "opposite" the individual; it is what every individual means when he says "we". But this "we" does not come into being because a large number of individual people who say "I" to themselves subsequently come together and decide to form an association. The interpersonal functions and relations that we express by grammatical particles such as "I", "you", "he", "she", "we" and "they" are interdependent. None of them has any existence without the others. And the "we" function includes all the others. Measured against what it refers to, everything one can call "I" or even "you" is only a part.

And this fact, that each "I" is irrevocably embedded in a "we", finally makes it clear why the intermeshing of the actions, plans and purposes of many "I"s constantly gives rise to something which has not been planned, intended or created by any individual. As is known, this permanent feature of social life was given its first historical interpretation by Hegel. He explains it as a "ruse of reason". But what is involved is neither a ruse nor a product of reason. The long-term planning of individuals, compared to the multiplicity of individual purposes and wishes within the totality of a human network, and particularly compared to the continuous interweaving of individual actions and purposes over many generations, is always extremely limited. The interplay of the actions, purposes and plans of many people is not itself something intended or planned, and is ultimately immune to planning. The "ruse of reason" is a tentative attempt, still swathed in day-dreaming, to express the fact that the autonomy of what a person calls "we" is more powerful than the plans and purposes of any individual "I". The interweaving of the needs and intentions of many people subjects each individual among them to compulsions that none of them has intended. Over and over again the deeds and works of individual people, woven into the social net, take on an appearance that was not premeditated. Again and again, therefore, people stand before the outcome of their own actions like the apprentice magician before the spirits he has conjured up and which, once at large, are no longer in his power. They look with astonishment at the convolutions and formations of the historical flow which they themselves constitute but do not control.

This is true of the simplest forms of relationship between people. For example, that fact that two different people strive for one and the same social opportunity, whether it be a piece of land or the same commodity, the same market or the same social position, gives rise to something that neither of them has intended: a competitive relationship with its specific laws, or, as the case may be, a rise or fall in prices. In this way, through the intermeshing of the closely related wishes or plans of many individuals, monopoly mechanisms come into play, advancing into wider and wider areas. Thus, for example, the disorderly monopoly of violence exercised by a whole class of freely competing feudal lords slowly gives rise, in the course of centuries, to a private, hereditary, central monopoly of force, and finally the centre of a state apparatus controllable by wide sections of the population. The same applies to the increasing division of functions. It too, as it now appears retrospectively to the observer – as a continuous change of human relationships in a certain direction over centuries – was certainly not planned or intended by any individual person or by many people together. No doubt, all the particular social instruments and institutions that gradually take on sharper contours, without being planned, in the course of such a process – urban settlements, machines or whatever they may be – are, from a certain time on, gradually incorporated more consciously into the aims and plans of individual people. Moreover, in the course of western history the sector of society open to planning grows larger and larger. But all these instruments and institutions, though built into the short-term purposes of many individual people and groups, tend at the same time, when considered over long stretches of time, always in a single direction that no individual person or group has wished or planned. In the same way, in the course of history, a change in human behaviour in the direction of civilization gradually emerged from the ebb and flow of events. Every small step on this path was determined by the wishes and plans of individual people and groups; but what has grown up on this path up to now, our standard of behaviour and our psychological make-up, was certainly not intended by individual people. And it is in this way that human society moves forward as a whole; in this way the whole history of mankind has run its course:

> From plans arising, yet unplanned
> By purpose moved, yet purposeless.

Notes

1 It is not entirely easy to explain what social structures and regularities are unless one is able to illustrate them by examples from social life itself, by detailed studies firmly based on experience. Owing to restricted space, that has not been possible here. I can only refer to the various analyses of social processes and regularities to be found in my study *The Civilizing Process* (vol. I, New York, 1978; vol. II, Oxford, 1982). Underlying them, but unstated, are the same ideas which are stated in more general form here.

2 On this and the following ideas cf. *The Civilizing Process*, vol. I, ch. 2, and vol. II, pp. 229ff: "Towards a theory of civilizing processes".

3 R. M. Rilke, from: *Sämtliche Werke*, Vol. I, Frankfurt/Main 1962, pp. 316–17:

> I am but one of your most humble monks
> looking from my cell out into life,
> further removed from people than from things
>   . . .
>
> Think me not presumptuous if I say:
> No one really lives his life.
> People are accidents, voices, fragments,
> fears, banalities, many petty joys,
> even as children wrapped up in disguise,
> adult as masks; as faces – mute.
>
> I often think: there must be treasuries
> where all these many lives are stored
> like armour or like litters, cradles,
> that never carried someone truly real,
> lives like empty clothes that cannot stand
> alone and, sinking, cling against
> the strong walls made of vaulted stone.

And when at evening I walked
out of my garden, full of weariness,
I know that all the stretching paths
lead to the arsenal of unlived things.
No tree is there, as if the land lay down
and as about a prison hangs the wall,
windowless in its sevenfold ring.
And its gates, with iron clasps
warding off those who seek to pass
and all its bars are made by human hands.

4　The situation we come across here in the relation of individual to society, person to person, has a certain similarity to the one which Goethe so frequently expressed regarding the relation of man to nature. Consider the following two poems (from Goethe, *Selected Poems*, London, 1983):

Epirrhema

You must, when contemplating nature,
Attend to this, in each and every feature:
There's nought outside and nought within
For she is inside out and outside in.
Thus will you grasp, with no delay,
The holy secret, clear as day.
　　　　　　　(trans. Christopher Middleton)

True Enough: To the Physicist

"Into the core of Nature" –
O Philistine –
"No earthly mind can enter."
The maxim is fine:
But have the grace
To spare the dissenter,
Me and my kind.
We think: in every place
We're at the centre.
"Happy the mortal creature
To whom she shows no more
Than the outer rind",
For sixty years I've heard your sort announce.

It makes me swear, though quietly;
To myself a thousand times I say:
All things she grants, gladly and lavishly;
Nature has neither core
Nor outer rind,
Being all things at once.
It's yourself you should scrutinise to see
Whether you're centre or periphery.
                    (trans. Michael Hamburger)

5 Here too lies the key to understanding the relation of civilization to human
   nature: the civilizing process is made possible by the fact that a person's self-
   regulation in relation to other beings and things, his or her "psyche", is not
   restricted by reflexes and innate automatisms to the same extent as, for
   example, the digestion. It is made possible by the peculiar adaptability and
   transformability of these self-regulatory functions. It is set in motion and
   kept in motion by specific changes in human communal life, a transformation
   of human relations operating in a very definite direction, an autonomous
   movement of the network of interdependent human individuals.

Part II

Problems of Self-consciousness
and the Image of Man
(1940s–1950s)

Wishful and Fear-inspired Self-images of Human Beings as Individuals and Society

I

Everyone knows what is meant when the word "society" is used, or at least, everyone thinks he knows. One generation passes the word on to another like a coin whose value is known and whose content no longer needs to be tested. If one person says "society" and another hears it, they understand each other without difficulty.

But do we really understand each other?

Society, as we know, is all of us; it is a lot of people together. But a lot of people together in India and China form a different kind of society than in America or Britain; the society formed by many individual people in Europe in the twelfth century was different from that in the sixteenth or the twentieth century. And although all these societies certainly consisted and consist of nothing other than many individuals, the change from one form of living together to another was clearly unplanned by any of these individuals. At least, it cannot be discovered that any person in the twelfth or even the sixteenth century worked deliberately towards the societies of our day, which take the form of urbanized, highly industrialized nation states. What kind of a formation is it, this "society" that we form together, yet which has not been intended or planned as it is now by any of us, or even all of us together, which only exists if a large number of people exist, which only continues to function if many individual

A few passages in the following text, particularly at the beginning of the first and third sections, comprise a direct revision of Part I of this volume people want and do certain things, yet the structure of which, its great historical transformations, clearly do not depend on the intentions of particular people?

If one considers the answers given to these and suchlike questions today, one is confronted, in broad terms, with two large opposed camps. One section of people approaches socio-historical formations as if they had been designed, planned and created, as they now stand before the retrospective observer, by a number of individuals or bodies. Although individuals within this general camp may at some level be aware that their kind of explanation is not quite adequate, no matter how they twist their ideas to fit the facts the conceptual model to which they are tied remains that of the rational and deliberate creation of a work – such as a building or a machine – by individual people. When they have particular social institutions before them, parliaments, police, banks, taxes, books or whatever it may be, to explain them they look for the people who first conceived the idea of such institutions or first put the idea into practice. If they are dealing with a literary *genre*, they look for the writer who gave the others a model. When they encounter social formations where this kind of explanation is difficult, language or the state, for example, they at least proceed *as if* these social formations could be explained in the same way as the others, the ones deliberately produced by individual people for a specific purpose. They may, for example, believe the existence of language to be sufficiently explained by noting its function as a means of communication between people, or that of states by arguing that the purpose of a state is the upholding of order, as if in the course of mankind's history language or the organization of people in the form of a state had at some time been created for this specific purpose by individual people as a result of rational thought. And often enough, when confronted by social phenomena that clearly cannot be explained according to this model, for example, the evolution of artistic styles or the civilizing process, their thinking comes to a halt. They stop asking questions.

In the opposite camp this approach to historical and social

formations is often treated with contempt. Here the human being as an individual hardly plays any part. The thought models used here are mainly modes of explanation drawn from the pure or applied sciences. But as so often when conceptual models are transferred from one field to another, the scientific models tend to take on a metaphysical character which, depending on the needs and preferences of their users, can have the flavour rather of a religion of reason or of a mystical faith. By and large, one can distinguish two main trends within this camp. Common to both is the endeavour to explain socio-historical formations and processes as the necessary products of the working of anonymous, supra-individual forces that are almost totally immune to human intervention. But the exponents of the other view stress the eternal recurrence of the same forms in societies, while their opponents assert the irrevocable change of societies – or of human society altogether – in a particular direction.

The first group generally conceive social processes as cycles that are inescapable and recur more or less automatically. Their models are usually taken from biology. They see a society as a kind of supra-individual organic entity which advances ineluctably through youth, maturity and age towards its death. Spengler's and Toynbee's social cosmologies are examples of this cyclical mode of thinking. But variations on this stationary notion of supra-individual social entities are widespread; they are to be found in various shades and disguises not only in scholarly books but in popular thought. One need only recall the common turn of phrase which suggests the idea, without one's always being conscious of it, that certain societies are possessed of a common, supra-individual spirit – the "spirit" of Greece for the ancient Greeks, the "spirit" of France for the French. Or one might think of the belief, widespread earlier, that a regular cycle of economic booms and slumps or the eternal recurrence of war and peace was the expression of a natural order of things, which ran its course in a way which could not be influenced by any deeper human insight into its causes or by human actions enlightened by such insight.

The exponents of the other main trend within this camp also

start out from the idea of an automatic, immutable social process. But they stress that this process advances irrevocably in a particular direction. They accommodate the recurrent rhythm within a strictly directed course which knows no recurrence. They see a kind of conveyor belt before them, on which each product automatically approaches perfection, or a kind of one-way street in which everyone is forced to advance in the same direction.

Sometimes, most obviously in Hegel, this manner of thinking finds expression in a kind of historical pantheism: a World Spirit, or God Himself, it then seems, embodies itself not in the static world of Spinoza but in the moving historical world, and serves to explain its order, its periodicity and its purpose.

Others make a strenuous attempt to bring the vision of a supra-individual social process moving inexorably in a particular direction down to earth from the realms of metaphysics by making it open to empirical investigation. Comte and Marx, each in his own way, are representatives of this attempt at a relatively early stage. Theirs is a grandiose vision, but it still floats midway between heaven and earth. Comte draws attention to a particular sequence of human thought processes; he sees it as the main key to understanding the socio-historical process. In all areas of human thought and action, he teaches, three stages, with numerous transitions and mixtures, can be discerned. They are so connected that the second necessarily emerges from the first and the third from the second. There is an anthropocentric religious stage, in which the hopes and fears of mankind are condensed into a socially pre-ordained belief in wish-fulfilling or punitive spirits; a metaphysical-philosophical stage when abstract concepts like "nature", "reason" or "spirit" form a different pantheon of metaphysical entities; and finally a scientific-positive stage when all ideas, all concepts and theories become undogmatically corrigible by systematic research and verifiable by application. Marx focuses attention on a sequence of economic relations, also seen as ineluctable, which for him represents the prime mover of socio-historical development and the main key to understanding it. In the course of this automatic development of economic relations, he teaches, a gradually diminishing group of owners of the means of production stands opposed to a gradually increasing group of propertyless persons, until finally, after a predictable series of inescapable social explosions, the propertyless poor gain the upper hand. Both Comte and Marx adhere more closely than most of their philosophical predecessors to a number of observable and verifiable facts. But they both suffer badly from inflated generalizations and a craving for necessity. Their generalizations often go far beyond the supporting facts. They usually read off from what is open to their observation only what they want to see, and they pronounce necessary whatever they find desirable. They prove to themselves, and attempt to prove to us, that socio-historical development must necessarily move in the direction in which they wish it to move. They integrate partial social processes that can actually be observed into a boldly painted total picture of the past and future development of mankind, a picture which reflects the direction of their hopes and fears. And the same applies to the whole army of those who proclaim not only a partial progress (that can indeed be observed in many areas) but the automatic advance of society in the direction of continuous progress – as it also applies to those who declare the rhythmical rise and fall of human societies (which can actually be observed here and there) to be an ineluctable law of human history. They all talk of human society as a supra-individual entity to whose laws human beings are powerlessly subject, as the Greeks were subject to the inescapable will of fate.

While for people of the opposite persuasion individual actions are at the centre of interest, and while in that quarter the phenomena that cannot be explained in terms of individual planning and creation are more or less lost to view, interest here is focused on just what the other camp finds difficult to grasp, such as modes of thought, artistic styles, economic systems or institutions. And while the first camp really fails to explain the link between the actions, thoughts and goals of individuals and such social formations, it is no less obscure how their adversaries make the connection in the opposite direction, from the social to the individual. They use scientific models to explain social formations by anonymous mechanical forces, or pantheistic-religious models to explain them by supra-individual spiritual powers.

But undoubtedly difficulties of this kind are not only encountered when studying historical and social facts in the narrower sense of the word. They are no less apparent when one is trying to understand people and society in terms of psychical functions. In the science that concerns itself with facts of this kind we find on one hand a tendency which treats the single individual as something that can be completely isolated. Scholars of this kind seek to illuminate the structure of the psychical functions of the individual independently of his relations to all other people, and they attempt to explain social phenomena, political and economic systems, languages, family types, mental structures or whatever it may be as a kind of mosaic resulting from the actions and psychical functions of individual people. On the other hand we find a socio-psychological approach whose problem and theories cannot be readily connected to a psychology based on the isolated individual. The members of this camp, rather like the corresponding camp in the other social sciences, sometimes attribute to whole societies a soul of their own beyond the individual souls, an *anima collectiva* or a "group mind". And even if they do not go quite so far, scholars are often content to treat socio-psychological phenomena as the sum or, what really comes to the same thing, the average of the behaviour of many individuals. Society then appears simply as an agglomeration of many individuals, the statistical determinant of attitudes and actions, instead of an indispensable aid (rather than a goal) and the most important evidence available to socio-psychological research. And however the different trends in individual and social psychology may proceed in detail, from this angle too the connection between the subject matter of both remains more or less mysterious. Often enough, it seems as if individual and social psychology are two entirely separable disciplines. And the questions of each are framed from the outset in a manner which suggests that there is in reality an unbridgeable gulf between the individual and society.

Wherever one looks, one comes across the same antinomies: we have a certain traditional idea of what we are as individuals. And we have a more or less distinct idea of what we mean when we say "society". But these two ideas, the consciousness we have of ourselves as society on one hand and as individuals on the other, never entirely coalesce. No doubt, we are aware at the same time that such a gulf between individuals and society does not exist in reality. Every human society consists of separate individuals, and every human individual only becomes human by learning to act, speak and feel in the society of others. Society without individuals or the individual without society is an absurdity. But if we try to reconstruct in thought what we live daily, gaps and fissures constantly appear in our train of thought as in a jigsaw puzzle the pieces of which refuse to form a complete image.

What we lack, let us be clear about it, are conceptual models and, beyond them, a total vision with the aid of which our ideas of human beings as individuals and as societies can be better harmonized. We cannot, it seems, make it clear to ourselves how it is possible for each individual person to be something unique, different from all others; a being who in a certain manner feels, experiences and does what no other person does; a self-contained being, and at the same time a being existing for others and among others, with whom he or she forms societies of changing structure, with histories that have been intended or brought about by none of the people constituting them in the way they actually unfold over centuries, and without which the individual could neither remain alive as a child nor learn to speak, think, love or behave as a human being.

II

When a doctor finds himself confronted with a patient whose symptoms are contradictory and incomprehensible, he will probably cast about in his mind for explanations that fit the case in the light of his previous knowledge.

What is the situation here? Is it possible that the difficulties we have in harmonizing the prevalent notions of people as individuals and people as societies are rooted in the nature of these entities, in the "thing in itself", in "people in society" as an object of human reflection? Or do the reasons for the difficulties lie rather in the modes of thought we normally use to decipher ourselves as objects of thought. In the transition from the cool, impartial manner of thought and observation in the realm of inanimate nature characteristic of the natural sciences as compared to magical or mythical modes, to a cooler and more impartial mode of thinking and observing with regard to the human world, we must climb to a new level of self-awareness. May the problems that arise in many areas when one thinks about the problems of the human universe have something to do with the fact the solving of such problems demands a breaking away from traditional forms of self-consciousness, from familiar and highly prized self-images? May they be linked to the fact that to overcome such problems in thought as in action a radical revision of our image of man is needed?

There is much reason to believe that the specific mode of life in industrialized nation states is linked to very specific types of image of man and of individual self-consciousness which differ clearly from those of other social groups, or of the same group in the past. Is it possible that the difficulties and contradictions that come to light in thinking about the relation of individual and society are connected to specific modes of life of these particular social groups? And that types of human image which reflect the state of self-consciousness of complex urban societies are not quite appropriate to what we actually are as people in society?

There is no doubt that in complex societies the influence of modes of thought and behaviour that have proved their worth in the rise of the natural sciences and the manipulation of inanimate nature, make themselves felt far beyond their original sphere. But perhaps modes of thought and behaviour of this type are not quite adequate to come to terms with subject matter such as the relation of individual and society. And in that case it might well be possible for the inadequacy of the modes of thinking based on the classical natural sciences to reinforce the tendency of people to seek a welcome refuge in pre-scientific, magical-mythical notions of themselves.

Perhaps it is somewhat more difficult for people to contemplate and analyse themselves unobstructed by their own wishes and fears than it is for them to lift the veil concealing inanimate nature. It is well and good for philosophers to call to us down the centuries: "Know thyself!", but perhaps most people, hearing this injunction, will think and feel: "We don't want to know too much about that."

On the other hand, of course, it is also possible that we have so little ability to withstand the catastrophes of history that have annihilated both life and meaning, and to diminish the suffering which human beings cause each other, just because we are unwilling to part with the fantasies with which we have traditionally embellished our existence. We are, indeed, swept on by the course of human history like the passengers of a train that is rushing along faster and faster without a driver and is entirely uncontrollable by its occupants. No one knows where the journey is taking him or when the next collision will come, or what can be done to bring the train under control. Is our ability to control our destiny as people in society as inadequate as it is simply because we find it extraordinarily difficult to think what lies behind the masks born of desire and fear with which we are smothered, and to see ourselves as we are? And is our ability to pierce these protective fantasies so slight because our ability to control the constant threats to human groups by other groups in the course of history is still so undeveloped? Is it so difficult for us to exclude the effects of our agitation, our wishful and fearful images, from our thinking about human beings, because we are so helplessly surrounded by the dangers which, in one form or another, human beings constitute for each other? And are we only able to ward off these dangers, to make our helplessness in face of the recurrent catastrophes of history bearable, by concealing them, by expelling them from consciousness? Finally, does not this veiling of reality by a tissue of thought in which the results of factual observation are still shot through with illusory material, contribute to our inability to master the endless destruction of groups of human beings by others?

Such connections between the proportions of fantasy and reality in human notions and the ability of people to control the area of existence to which these notions pertain are not, of course, new. In earlier times, as we know, human experience in the sphere of natural events was much less adequate to the facts, and the course of these events was less controllable. And in this case, too, was not one thing the cause and the other the effect? Here, too, the movement circulated endlessly through a two-way connection.

Think, for example, of the use of magic. On one hand, as a form of thought and action it helps people to gain control within their own fantasy of processes which as yet they are hardly able to influence in reality – for example, the flourishing or withering of their fields and herds, lightning, rain, pestilence and other natural processes which deeply affect their lives. The fantasy thoughts and acts of magic help people to alleviate an otherwise unbearable situation in which they are wholly exposed, like small children, to mysterious and uncontrollable forces. Magic formulae and practices make it possible to cover up and banish from consciousness the terrors of this situation, the total insecurity and vulnerability it brings with it, the ever-present prospect of suffering and death. They make people who use them feel they have gained insight into the nature of things and power over their course. And if, as usually happens, the belief in their effectiveness is shared by the members of a particular group, it becomes so strongly entrenched that it is very difficult to eradicate. Consequently, this binding of thought and action to magical-mythical forms of experience steeped in fantasy and feeling always makes it difficult, and sometimes impossible, for people to use more realistic forms of knowledge and behaviour to reduce the threat from uncontrolled natural events, and to bring such events more completely under their control.

We do not need to discuss here how people have managed to break out of the vicious circle operating in this area of their lives, as regards their relation to events in the sphere of physical nature. It may be enough to say that this problem is one of the main focal points in the development of an epistemological theory in which the two streams of the classical philosophical theory of cognition on one hand and the sociological theory of knowledge on the other are reconciled. In its manner of posing problems this new theory takes no less account of the acquisition of knowledge of human phenomena in the form of the social sciences than of the gaining of knowledge of extra-human natural phenomena in the form of the natural sciences. The basic figure of the vicious circle is to be found in both spheres. But in the sphere of human-social existence it occurs on a different level than in that of natural events or, more precisely, in the situation of the people acting and thinking with regard to this sphere. This is, at least, the case in complex industrial societies, where the fantasy content of public thinking about natural events is relatively slight and the controllability of such events relatively great. In thinking about the problems of human communal life and in coping with such problems, the force of the old *circulus vitiosus* is far more strongly felt. Events in this sphere are less controllable; thought contains a greater element of fantasy and feeling; and it is more difficult to approach the problems in a relatively unprejudiced or, as we normally say, "rational" manner.

The traditional idea of a "reason" or "rationality" with which each person is equipped by nature as an innate peculiarity of the human species, which illuminates the whole environment like a lighthouse (unless there is a malfunction), does not conform at all well to the observable facts. Commonplace as the idea is today, it is itself part of an image of man in which verifiable observations are strongly admixed with fantasies born of wishes and fears. The assumption that human thought functions automatically according to eternal laws at all times and in all social situations, as long as it is free of disturbance, is an amalgam of factual knowledge and a wishful ideal. Contained in it is a moral demand (with which one has no need to argue as such) masquerading as a fact. And as long as we accept this kind of self-consciousness and this human image, with all their masks and impurities, as something to be taken for granted, we can hardly come to grips with the problem under discussion here. Even if we consider only present-day industrial societies, the inadequacy of such notions is obvious enough. Few things are as characteristic of the situation and the make-up of people in such societies as the relatively high degree of "rationality" or "respect for the facts" which they exhibit – or, more exactly, the adequacy of their thought and the controllability of events – with regard to physical nature, and the relative lack of both with regard to their own social life.

And these differences of the human situation in the broad field of society are mirrored in the different stage of development of the corresponding sciences, a discrepancy which in turn contributes to the perpetuation of these social differences. The natural sciences normally influence public thinking on natural events by holding back affective notions, particularly through the practical success of their application to technical problems. The social sciences, for their part, still tend to be strongly influenced in their basic ideas and their conceptual procedure by the affective images and ideas which are prevalent in the public sphere of their societies. Even concepts and research methods that have proved themselves appropriate in the natural sciences often take on a magical flavour when uncritically adopted by the social sciences. They give the people using them a feeling of insight and power without actually conferring such insight or power to the same extent.

Sciences are not carried on in a vacuum. It is therefore

pointless to build up a doctrine of science which proceeds as if that were the case. In its causes and effects the state of development of the human sciences, as of the natural sciences, is characteristic of a specific human situation.

In relation to natural events, more than to socio-historical developments, human beings have been able to break out of the vicious circle which makes the degree of uncertainty and threat faced by men dependent on the adequacy of human thought and action, and vice versa. In the sphere of natural events, people have gradually managed, over the centuries, to pen back the threats and to develop models of thought and action which possess a relatively high degree of fearlessness, impartiality and appropriateness. What we call "the sciences" are a characteristic element of this situation.

However, in the realm of human and social relationships, people are more inextricably caught up in the vicious circle. They are less able to deal adequately in thought and deed with the problems facing them the more their lives are threatened, in the area of these problems, by uncontrollable dangers, tensions and conflicts, and dominated by the resultant fears, hopes and wishes. And they are less able to withstand the dangers, conflicts and threats to which they are exposed, the less objective they are in their thoughts and actions, the more susceptible to feeling and fantasy. In other words, the human sciences and the general ideas people have of themselves as "individuals" and as "societies" are determined, in their present form, by a situation in which human beings as individuals and as societies import into each other's lives considerable and largely uncontrollable dangers and fears. And these forms of knowledge and thought about people contribute in their turn to the constant reproduction of such dangers and fears. They are a cause as well as an effect of this situation. As happened earlier in relation to natural events, here too, in keeping with the high degree of insecurity, danger and vulnerability prevailing in this area, collective fantasies and semi-magical customs have specific functions. Here too they help to make the uncertainty of a situation which people are unable to master more bearable to them. They protect people from a full awareness of dangers in face of which they are powerless. They serve as weapons of defence and attack in their conflicts with each other. They make societies more cohesive and give their members a feeling of power over events over which, in reality, they often have little control. To expose them as fantasies is dangerous, or at least is felt to be a dangerous and perhaps hostile act. Their social effectiveness depends in good measure on their being thought of as realistic ideas, not as fantasies. And as they possess a social effectiveness as collective fantasies, they themselves form – unlike many purely personal fantasies – a part of social reality.

But what was said earlier about the social function of mythical ideas and magical actions in relation to natural events also applies to their function in the sphere of social life. Here, too, affect-charged modes of thought and action contribute to a failure to master the dangers and fears they are supposed to dispel, and perhaps even reinforce them. The collective conviction of their objective adequacy gives them a solidity and permanence which, as in the case of the magical notions about nature in simpler societies, cannot be weakened simply by pointing to contradictory facts.

This is seen, for example, in national ideologies and the conviction of the special merit, the greatness and superiority of one's own national tradition explicitly or implicitly linked to them. On one hand they help to bind together the members of a state and to close their ranks when danger threatens; on the other they serve to stoke up the fires of conflict and tension between nations, and to keep alive, or even increase, the dangers which nations seek to ward off with their help. Often enough values which represent the essence of what gives life purpose and meaning contribute to the constant renewal of tendencies destructive of life and meaning, which in their turn reinforce the values that serve as a defence against these threats.

III

The same applies to the current notions of what are called "individual" and "society". It applies in particular to their relation to each other. Dangers and fears of the most diverse kinds affect the discussion of this relation. They too bear on the situation of the people involved in the discussion; and the less aware one is of this situation the stronger is their tacit influence on the course of the discussion; the parties become less impartial and thought loses its independence.

For example, it is not entirely without significance for the discussion of such problems that, within the broad field of society, disputes are taking place between parties, classes and states which legitimize themselves by social professions of faith based on diametrically opposed *valuations* of "individual" and 'society". In their most popular form, the professions of one side present the "individual" as a means and the "social whole" as the supreme value and purpose, while the others regard "society" as the means and "individuals" as the supreme value and purpose. And in both cases these ideals and goals of political thought and action are often presented as facts. What one side says *should* be is thought and spoken of as if it *is*. For example, members of a group in which it is loyal to demand and wish that the claims of the state or other organization *should* have precedence over those of individuals, may believe they perceive that social collectives of this or that kind *are* actually, at all times, more real and carry greater weight than the individuals who form them. And members of groups in which it is loyal to demand and wish that the claims of individuals *should* have priority over those of the group, often believe they can observe that individuals are the true reality, that which actually exists, while societies are something that comes afterwards, something less real and perhaps even a mere figment of thought, an abstraction. In both cases what is demanded and desired merges in consciousness with what observably is. And in keeping with the strength of the disturbances and tensions to which the holders of such opposed views are exposed within their social context, it is usually the former that gain the upper hand.

It is, therefore, no simple undertaking to evolve, untroubled by such professions of faith, conceptual models of "the individual" and "society" more in harmony with what *is*, what is proved to be fact by systematic observation and reflection. Such an undertaking might, in the long term, help to loosen the screw of the vicious circle whereby a lack of control over events results in a permeation of thought by affective fantasies and a lack of rigour in thinking about these events, which in turn leads to still less control over the events. In the short term it may well seem futile and pointless to try to disentangle the relation of "individual" and "society", as it actually *is* at all times from its sheath of temporary images engendered by wish and fear, such as the mutually hostile doctrines of "individualism" and "collectivism".

At present words such as "individual", "society", "personality", "collective", being ideological weapons in the power struggles of various parties and states, are so permeated with emotive content that it is difficult to extricate their factural core from the desires and fears of those involved in the struggles. Just as, earlier, magic formulae were used to heal sicknesses that could not yet be adequately diagnosed, today people often use magic doctrines as means of solving human and social problems, without troubling to establish a diagnosis uninfluenced by desire and fear. And in such doctrines words like "individual" and "society" play a considerable role as symbols and passwords.

Thus the word "individual", for example, may arouse negative feelings in people to whom the doctrine of "individualism" is distasteful. They may associate the word with the image of ruthless, brutal individuals bent on oppressing others and enriching themselves at their expense. Or it may arouse a negative feeling in them because they regard the subordination of the individual to the state or some other social unit – dedication to the nation, solidarity with one's class, submission to the commandments of the church or self-sacrifice for a racial group – as the fulfilment of their individual life or the highest human ideal altogether. Feelings of this kind may then condense into the mythological idea that social units like nations, races or classes actually have an existence prior to and independently of all individuals, that there are, so to speak, *societies without individuals*.

And conversely: for some the word "individual" may be associated with pride in their self-sufficient position in society. It may symbolize what the individual person can achieve independently of all others and in competition with them, through his or her own energy and merit. In it all the positive valuations of their ideal, "individualism", may re-echo. Or it may convey to them an image of great, creative personalities whom they revere, whom they seek to emulate and with whom, in a corner of their souls, they may identify themselves. "Society" may mean for them what makes everyone equal, what stands in the way of the self-realization or advancement of the individual personality. The image they associate with this word may be of an inert mass of grey, indistinguishable people which threatens to push everyone down to the same level. They may see it as the essence of everything that stands in the way of individual fulfilment, preventing someone from expressing what is in him – in short, as what limits and threatens freedom more than anything else. Feelings of this kind may condense into the idea that in the beginning there actually were isolated individuals – *individuals without society* – who only related together and formed societies at a later stage.

In short, what one understands by "individual" and "society" still depends to a large extent on the form taken by what people wish for and fear. It is extensively conditioned by ideals charged with positive feelings and anti-ideals charged with negative feelings. People experience "individual" and "society" as things which are separate and often opposed – not because they can actually be observed as separate, opposed entities, but because they associate these words with different and often opposite feelings and emotive values. These emotive patterns operate as selective templates before the mind's eye; they determine to a good extent which facts are perceived as essential and which are discarded as unimportant when one thinks about individual people and the societies they form together. And if, as often happens today, this selective mechanism functions in such a way that the individual and social aspects of people are perceived and valued as different, they can easily be ascribed a kind of special, different existence.

IV

In practical life, in one's direct dealings with people, it usually seems quite obvious that these different aspects of human beings are inseparable. It seems quite natural that someone is this unique person called Hans-Heinz Weber, who is at the same time a German, a Bavarian, a citizen of Munich, a Catholic, a publisher, married and father of three children. The lens of attention can be given a wider or narrower focus; it can be focused on what distinguishes a person from all others as something unique; or on what links him to others, his relations to and dependence on others; and finally on the specific changes and structures of the network of relationships of which he is a part.

We have reached a stage in the development of language and thought where it is possible to classify in general terms the different levels focused on by a different adjustment of the lens, distinguishing them by different expressions. It is always the same people that are seen; but one setting of the lens shows them as individuals, while a larger or smaller setting shows them as social units – as families, nations, or perhaps as firms, professional associations and social classes. As a first approach to the problem this is simple enough; and if it were possible to study it as a detached and impartial observer, one could proceed further from this point.

But in the course of the power struggles and tensions between the exponents of opposed social ideals these expressions take on the additional significance of emotive symbols. The question as to the nature of the relation between what is classified as "individual" and "society" is obscured by the question which of them is more valuable. And as, in the conflict of ideals, one is usually valued far more highly than the other, often being seen as positive while the other is negative, the two terms are used as if they referred to two different things or two different people. One speaks of "individual" *and* "society" in the same way as one speaks of salt *and* pepper or mother *and* father. In thought and speech we use two concepts by which human phenomena from two inseparable planes of observation are classified as if they referred to two different entities, one of which could exist without the other. This, the idea of the separate existence of the two, of individuals who exist in some sense beyond society, or societies which exist in some sense beyond individuals, is in fact one of the tacit assumptions common to the two adversaries in the struggle of the "individualists" and the "collectivists", or whatever they may call themselves. It is one of the untested and undisputed bases of their struggle.

As a starting point for a discussion of the question of the nature of the individual and social aspects of human beings, this use of the words "individual" and "society" invariably leads thought down blind alleys made up of insoluble pseudo-problems. The idea it suggests, the image of two different entities separated by a broad chasm or an unbridgeable antithesis, is responsible in large measure for all the endless discussions on the question which was "there" first, "individual" or "society" – variations on the old conundrum of chicken and egg – or the other question as to which determines which: "Must one proceed from 'individuals' in order to understand 'societies', or from social phenomena to explain individuals?" As the unquestioned basis of research this image lends support to the idea that the division of the human sciences into those which deal with individuals and those which deal with societies is more than a mere phase in the scientific division of labour which must lead sooner or later to connections and syntheses. It suggests that this is a division justified by the separate existence of the subject matter itself. It leads to the posing of confused historical questions, such as: "Is the driving force of historical change provided by great personalities or by impersonal social forces?" In other words, we have here a typical example of the way in which different valuations and feelings associated with different aspects or functions of the same subject matter condense, when the corresponding words are used, into the idea that we are in fact dealing with different subject matter. And since, in the course of such controversies, one is often forced into attributing a higher reality to what one values more highly, one finds oneself involved in discussions about the reality of concepts reminiscent of those of the scholastics: "Are social relations the only reality and individuals merely a product of the social environment?" "Are individuals the true reality and societies a mere figure of speech?" "Or are they both real and stand in a reciprocal relationship to each other?"

If the matter is stated like this so that one is fully aware of what is at stake, it is not difficult to grasp that all the modes of thought and speech that lead one to use the terms "individual" and "society" as if they referred to two separate, independent entities – not excluding the notion of their "reciprocal relationship" – are very crude and not especially adequate. And if one takes account of our historical knowledge of European societies of earlier periods or our knowledge of contemporary societies at an earlier stage of development, it is easily understood that the notion of such a division and antithesis between "individual" and "society", between the "self" and "the others", is by no means the universal, self-evident manner in which human beings perceive themselves that it often claims to be.

But however inadequate such modes of thought and speech may be as a means of explaining the general reality, as a means of expressing the experience of people in a particular historical epoch, of members of the most complex and individualized societies now existing, they are perfectly authentic and genuine. And however obvious the facts that one could point to to show that these forms of experience and the concepts corresponding to them are not very adequate to reality, for many people they carry a conviction which is unshaken by reference to facts.

Prevalent usage in speech and thought makes these concepts and many others relating to the human world very susceptible to affective loadings. Their meaning, therefore, is usually more indicative of the emotive state of the person using them than of the facts they refer to. And this emotive loading of thought and speech relating to events in the human world is not a sign of deficiencies in what is called – by a half-reifying, half-metaphysical term – "reason" or "understanding". The problem that faces us here is often obscured by the idea that people possess "reason" by nature, a reason that, like the light of a lighthouse, illuminates all the regions of life uniformly, provided it is not blocked by emotions as by passing clouds. The problem only emerges with its full significance if one takes account of the basic structural peculiarity of the human situation that has already been mentioned, the circular movement whereby the development of social control over a particular area of life is dependent on the rigour of thought about this area, and vice versa.

The social standard of control of the area we refer to as "natural events" is fairly high in industrial states, and the same is true of the self-control of thought and observation within this area. Here the insecurity of people has diminished noticeably in the course of the last centuries, as has the element of wish and fear in mental activity in this sphere. But in relation to large areas of the human world, especially its tensions and conflicts, both the standard of social control over events and that of self-control in thinking about them is considerably less. The mutual threats of people and particularly of states, and the resulting insecurity, are still very great, and the restraint of affects in thinking about this area is low, compared to that normal in relation to natural events.[1]

The intrusion of ideals and values arising from the power struggles within society and carrying a strong affective charge into apparently objective discussions on the relation of "individual" and "society" is one of many examples of this kind of two-way link. This is the vicious circle, the trap in which we are caught: it is very difficult to raise the standard of self-discipline, the restraint of wishes and fears – and thus the adequacy of ideas and observations – as long as there is a high level of conflict and tension between people and a low degree of control over them. And it is difficult to make such tensions and conflicts more amenable to human control as long as there is a high level of affectivity in the thought and perception pertaining to this area, and a low level of objectivity.

The notion that ideas and thought alone can serve as a starting point in loosening the screw of this vicious circle reminds us somewhat of the story of Baron Munchausen, who pulled himself out of the marsh by his own pigtail. For in all these matters what is important is not what this or that person may think. However rich or bold an individual's imagination may be, he can never move far away from the contemporary standard of thought and speech. He is bound to this standard if only by the linguistic instruments available to him. If he uses them in a manner which departs too far from the prevalent usage he ceases to be intelligible. His words forfeit their main function as instruments of communication between people. The potential for developing them by the individual may be considerable, but it is always limited. For ideas that cease to be communicable have no meaning. For this reason, what has been said here on the vicious circle relates first and foremost to the current *social* standard of thought and speech. That is what forms a kind of functional cycle with the social standard of control over the area of life in question. As long as the actual control is relatively limited and the thought heavily affect-charged and objectively inadequate, the two constantly reinforce each other. And the tendency to perpetuate the form they have once taken on makes it extremely difficult to set one in motion without pushing the other on in the same direction.

All the same – thinking probably helps to some extent.

The Thinking Statues

I

Discussion on the relation of individual and society are often based explicitly or implicitly on an idea that can be summarized as follows: "What can really be *seen* are individual people. Societies cannot be seen. They cannot be perceived with the senses. One cannot therefore say that they exist or are 'real' in the same sense or to the same degree as one can say it of the individual people forming them. In the end, everything one can say about social formations is based on observations of individual people and their utterances or products."

In keeping with this fundamental position, many people arrive at the conviction that all statements about social phenomena are really generalizations of observations made of individuals; and one sometimes hears the remark that not only *statements* about such phenomena but the phenomena themselves, societies and all individual social formations, are as such nothing but abstractions. "It is all very well", someone may say, "to present social formations simply as relations between individual people. But as only the latter can be perceived, is not everything that can be said about such relations deduced indirectly from observations of individual people? As relations as such cannot be directly perceived, how is it possible to investigate them? How, to adapt Kant's well-known question, are social sciences possible at all?"

In considering one of the fundamental problems of the social sciences, therefore, one encounters questions which have a certain kinship to problems of classical epistemology. In both cases the starting point of reflection is the idea that all our knowledge is primarily knowledge of individual bodies or at least of physical events that we perceive with the senses. One of the fundamental problems with which this confronts us is the question how we arrive at our knowledge of all relations between individual bodies that are not perceptible with the senses. In one case it is the question of the origin of our knowledge of relationships between individual people, in the other the question of the origin of our knowledge of relations between non-human objects and changes in them, for example, their relationship as cause and effect.

The similarity of the questions is by no means accidental. In both cases it is connected to a peculiar form of self-consciousness and of the image of man. But one is not usually aware of it as such, as a special variant of our consciousness of ourselves and others. It usually presents itself to the person concerned as something natural and universally human, as *the* form of human self-consciousness, the image that people have of themselves at all times.

One may be aware at the same time that there are and have been other ways of experiencing oneself and others. One may know that our own familiar form of self-consciousness, our image of man, emerges late in the history of mankind, at first slowly and for a relatively short period in limited circles of ancient society, and then in the so-called Renaissance in occidental societies. Nevertheless, it usually appears as the normal, healthy way of perceiving ourselves and others, which unlike others needs no explanation. Even today this image still seems so self-evident that it is difficult to detach it from its fixed place in one's own consciousness and to hold it out, as it were, as something new and astonishing.

On the other hand, as long as we are unable to do so we run the risk of encountering insuperable difficulties in solving both practical and theoretical questions, in both action and thought. To be sure, criticism of self-consciousness, the demand for a revision of the basic forms of perceiving oneself and others prevalent in our own society, will meet understandable resistance. The basic structure of the idea we have of ourselves and other people is a fundamental precondition of our ability to deal successfully with other people and, at least within the confines of our own society, to communicate with them. If it is called into question, our own security is threatened. What was certain becomes uncertain. One is like a person suddenly thrown into the sea, with no sight of dry land. Unquestioned assumptions, the basic structures of thought that we take over with the words of our language without further reflection, are among the indispensable means of orientation without which we lose our way, just as we lose the ability to orientate ourselves in space if the familiar signposts that determine what we expect to perceive turn out to be unreliable and deceptive. But without throwing oneself for a time into the sea of uncertainty one cannot escape the contradictions and inadequacies of a deceptive certainty.

It may help to throw the strangeness of our own image of ourselves and of man into sharper relief if we see it retrospectively, in the mirror of the image of self and man that was again and again fundamental to the struggle to solve the problem of knowledge over the centuries.

Let us consider, for example, the man who first posed, in a paradigmatic way, the problem of knowledge and cognition in more or less the form it has kept to our day, Descartes. The dictum associated with his name, "I think, therefore I am", has become a kind of slogan. But this dictum gives only a pale and misleading idea of the image of self and man underlying his meditations. To understand this basic conception we must recall at least the outlines of the process of thought, the period of doubt and uncertainty that he passed through before he found firm ground under his feet in the new certainty that the indubitable fact of one's own reflection also put the existence of one's own self beyond doubt.

He asked himself first whether there was anything of which one was absolutely certain, anything that could not be doubted under any circumstances. In social life, he realized, one had to accept many ideas as if they were the gospel, though they were anything but certain. Descartes therefore decided to set out in search of that which was absolutely certain, and to discard all conceptions on which there could be even the slightest doubt. "Everything I have learned," he said to himself, "everything I know, I have learned through or from sense perceptions. But can one really trust one's senses? Can I be certain that I am sitting here beside my warm stove in my dressing-gown, holding this piece of paper in my hand? Can I be quite certain that these are my hands and my body? Of course, I see my hands; I feel my body. But," said the dissenting voice of doubt, "are there not people who believe they are kings while in reality they are paupers? Are there not people who are convinced that their heads are of stoneware and their bodies of glass? Is it not possible that God has so arranged things that I *believe* I see heaven and earth, and *believe* I have a three-dimensional body, while in reality nothing of the kind exists? Or, if God has not done so, is it not possible that an evil spirit may be deluding me into thinking that I feel, see and hear all these things which in reality do not exist? One cannot", he told himself, "dismiss this possibility." And as he felt compelled in this way to reject one by one all ideas of himself and the world as dubious and unreliable, he finally succumbed, like other people under the unremitting pressure of doubt, to the blackest despair. There was nothing certain in the world, so it seemed to him, nothing that could not be doubted.

"I must therefore", he wrote, "take into account the possibility that heaven and earth, all forms in space, are nothing but illusions and fantasies used by an evil spirit to trap my credulity. I shall conceive that I myself have neither eyes nor hands, neither flesh, blood nor senses, but falsely believe I possess all of them."

Only after he had spent some time wandering in the tunnel of uncertainty and subjecting all his experiences to the trial by fire of his radical doubt did he see a faint gleam of light at the end. However doubt may have gnawed at him and threatened to destroy all certainty, there was, he discovered, one fact that could not be doubted: "Would it be possible", he asked, "for me finally to convince myself that I myself do not exist? No, I myself exist.

For I can convince myself that I am able to think something and to doubt it."

Here we reach the core of this peculiar form of self-consciousness: sense perceptions and therefore the knowledge of physical objects including one's own body, all that may be doubtful and deceptive. But one cannot doubt, Descartes concludes, that one doubts. "It is not possible for me to think that I do not think. And that I think is not possible unless I exist."

The conception of the human self that we come across here and the questions it implies are far more than the mental games of a particular philosopher. They are highly characteristic of the transition from a conception of human beings and the world with strong religious underpinning to secularized conceptions, a transition which was making itself felt in Descartes's day. This secularization of human thought and action was certainly not the work of an individual or a number of individuals. It was connected to specific changes affecting all relationships of life and power in occidental societies. Descartes's deliberations represent a typical step in this direction in an original version. They indicate in a paradigmatic manner the peculiar problems with which people found themselves confronted in thinking about themselves and the certainty of their image of themselves when the religious picture of self and world became an open target of doubt and lost its self-evident status. This basic picture that dispensed certainty, the notion people had of themselves as part of a divinely created universe, did not thereby disappear, but it lost its central and dominant position in thought. As long as it held this position, that which could be perceived by the senses or confirmed by thought or observation played at most a secondary part in people's questions, thoughts and perceptions. The questions which mattered most to them concerned something that, in principle, could not be discovered by observation with the aid of the sense organs, or by thought supported by that which people ascertained by a methodical use of eyes and ears. They concerned, for example, the destination of the soul or the purpose of men and beasts in the framework of divine creation. To questions of this kind people could only find an answer with the help of recognized authorities of one kind or another, holy writings or favoured men – in short, through direct or indirect revelation. Individual observations were of very little help, individual reflection only helped in so far as it presented itself as an interpretation of one of the sources of revelation. And people accordingly felt themselves to be part of an invisible spiritual realm. They could feel themselves embedded in a hierarchy of beings the lowest rung of which was formed by the plants and animals, the highest by the angels, the pinnacle being God Himself. Or they may have experienced themselves as a kind of microcosm whose destiny was closely bound to that of the macrocosm of creation. Whatever the particular form, it was a basic feature of this picture of man and the world that what could be perceived by the senses took on its meaning from something that could be discovered and confirmed neither by individual reflection nor by individual observations.

One precondition of Descartes's thinking was a certain relaxation, a loss of power by the social institutions which had been the custodians of this intellectual tradition. His thought reflects the growing awareness of his time that people were able to decipher natural phenomena and put them to practical use simply on the basis of their own observation and thought, without invoking ecclesiastical or ancient authorities. Because of the prior work of thinkers of classical antiquity this discovery appeared to the people of the time like a rediscovery. It was a rediscovery of themselves as beings who could attain certainty about events by their own thought and observation, without recourse to authorities. And it moved their own mental activity – reified by the term "reason" – and their own powers of perception into the foreground of their image of themselves.

II

Now that all these ideas are taken for granted it is, perhaps, not very easy to put oneself in the position of people living in the time when such experiences were a new development gradually intruding, not without powerful resistance, into human thought processes. But to remember an epoch when what is almost self-evident today still had the lustre and freshness of unfamiliarity throws into sharper relief some features of our own basic conceptions of ourselves and the world, conceptions which, through familiarity, normally remain below the threshold of clear consciousness. It makes us fully aware of the fact that the image which members of the pioneering European and American societies have of themselves today – an image of beings who understand events solely by the application of intelligence, by individual observation and thought – should not be taken for granted as something which exists a priori. It cannot be understood in isolation from the social situation of those who see themselves in this way. It evolved as a symptom of and a factor in a specific transformation which, like all such changes, simultaneously affected all the three basic co-ordinates of human life: the shaping and the position of the individual within the social structure, the social structure itself and the relation of social human beings to events in the non-human world. It may be easier to see in retrospect how closely this transition from a predominantly authoritarian mode of thinking to a more autonomous one, at least as regards natural events, was bound up with the more comprehensive advance of individualization in the fifteenth, sixteenth and seventeenth centuries in Europe. It formed a parallel to the transition from a more "external" conscience dependent on authorities to a more autonomous and "individual" one. One can see more clearly in retrospect how closely this new form of self-consciousness was linked to the growing commercialization and the formation of states, to the rise of rich court and urban classes and, not least, to the noticeably increasing power of human beings over non-human natural events.

In the course of these discoveries about natural events people found out new things about themselves. They not only learned increasingly how to gain certainty about natural events by methodical thought and observation; they also became increasingly aware of themselves as beings who were able to gain such certainty by their own individual observation and thought. Their image of the physical universe changed, and their image of themselves also changed. With regard to themselves, they were less inclined to accept the traditional image advanced by authorities. They examined themselves more carefully in the mirror of their consciousness, observed themselves, thought about human beings more consciously and systematically. In short, they climbed to a new level of self-consciousness. Both changes – in their image of the non-human universe and of themselves – were closely linked. And the Cartesian enquiry, the whole "epistemological" enquiry itself, was nothing other than an expression of this new human self-image.

III

That is not to say that the people undergoing these changes were aware of such changes in the same way as we are today, from a distance. From about the "Renaissance" on, the basic form of self-consciousness and the human image prevalent today slowly formed in a number of societies until they were taken for granted. The fact that we can now perceive this is itself an expression of the gradual advance to a further stage of self-consciousness. Another such expression is the fact that the form of self-consciousness that is taken for granted and now seems like a universally valid concept of man, can be perceived as something that has evolved by a certain process, in conjunction with the wider social context.

As compared to their medieval predecessors, the members of

European societies from the "Renaissance" on climbed to a new level of self-consciousness. They were increasingly able to see themselves as if from a distance, taking the sun as the centre of the universe instead of naively assuming the earth and thus themselves to be the centre. This "Copernican revolution" was highly characteristic of the new level of self-consciousness which these people slowly attained.

But as compared to that level of self-consciousness, we find ourselves today beginning here and there to climb to the next. We are learning to see our own image simultaneously in the mirror of self-consciousness and in another, larger and more distant mirror. As the rise of the natural sciences was earlier, today their rapid advance and the rise of the social and human sciences are both a driving force and a symptom of this change.

It would undoubtedly be preferable if one were able to speak simply of an enlargement of people's knowledge about them-selves. But although such a formulation would not be incorrect, it is not enough; it does not quite do justice to the facts. The process of acquiring knowledge, the constant increase in our knowledge of facts, the closer approximation of human ideas and procedures to what can be established as fact by critical observation, the whole change in our mode of experience over the generations – and thus in the course of an individual life – is not in all cases simply an extension in one dimension. We are not concerned only with a growing accumulation of factual knowledge, ideas or methods of thought or research that exist on the same plane like objects on a table.

There are also differences between *levels* of observation – comparable to those between the view one has of people in the street when one is among them, and the different view they offer when seen from the first floor of a house, from the fifth floor or even from an aeroplane. From time to time – for example, at the end of the "Middle Ages" or, in our own time, from the end of the eighteenth century or, analogously, in contemporary African or Asian societies – one can observe, accompanying the steady accumulation of social knowledge and a specific transformation of social life, this broader and higher perspective being attained, a perspective characteristic of a new level of consciousness.

The special difficulty which this state of affairs puts in the way of undertanding and description lies in the fact that the new perspective does not simply abolish perspectives from other levels of consciousness. The comparison with the viewpoints of the pedestrian and the aircraft pilot is a lame one. People are made in such a way that, to pursue the metaphor, they can experience themselves and others directly as pedestrians while at the same time watching themselves and others walking up and down the street from an upper floor of a building. And perhaps, at the same time, they can even make out their own figures from the pilot's viewpoint, both as they walk along the street and as they look down from the building.

Simpler societies – and children in all societies – still offer examples of people for whom the ability to see themselves and their companions from a distance, like spectators from the window of a building while at the same time walking along the street, is still quite unattainable. They have, of course, a consciousness of themselves and other people. But they still live and act in direct connection with others. They have no access to a form of experience and a range of ideas which enables people to experience themselves as something apart from and independent of their own group, as a person in a sense standing opposed to their group. They are not "individualized" in the sense in which the word can be used when applied to people of more complex societies. One might be tempted to say that they are conscious without being self-conscious. But although this formulation does touch on something significant in the situation in question, strictly speaking it is not quite adequate. For all the simpler societies still existing seem to have in their vocabularies, besides "we", concepts corresponding to our "I" and "you". One must consider the possibility, at least as a hypothesis, that there have been human groups in which even adults could not perform the act of self-distancing that is needed in order to speak of oneself as "I" and of others as "you". On the other hand, it is quite possible that people of many simple and even quite complex contemporary societies are unable to perform the further act of self-distancing that is needed in order to experience oneself not merely as "I" but as a possible "you" for others who say "I" of themselves.

The simplest examples of the many-layered nature of consciousness at the other end of human development so far are probably to be found in certain areas of literature. One might think of the development of the novel since the second half of the nineteenth century. In the prose writings of earlier centuries – and certainly not only in the *prose* writings – the writer was mainly preoccupied with telling the reader what people did, what happened. Gradually attention became concentrated not only on the narration of events but on how the people experienced them. The authors described a landscape, for example, and at the same time the so-called "inner landscape" in the narrower or broader sense of the term – *le paysage intérieur*. They described meetings between people and at the same time the "stream of consciousness" of the people as they met. But no matter what slogans were used, the change that found expression in literature was by no means confined to literature. The writers' special sensitivity enabled them, as a kind of vanguard of society, to perceive and express changes that were going on in the broad field of the societies in which they lived. If this had not been the case they would have found no readers who understood and appreciated them. These literary forms are indeed testimonies to the slow rise to a new level of consciousness that can be observed in a number of societies. And the present discussion is really nothing other than an attempt to carry forward the description of this further stage of self-consciousness and of the human image that is gradually rising above the horizon, in conjunction with further discoveries by people about themselves as individuals, societies and natural formations.

IV

One of the difficulties facing one in such an attempt is connected to the fact that as yet there are hardly any long-term investigations of such changes in the history of societies or of individuals. Nor are there convincing theoretical models of this development towards a multi-layered consciousness. Expressions like the "transition to a new level of consciousness" may perhaps have a somewhat Hegelian timbre for those familiar with that philosopher. One can say very generally that the words currently used when seeking a somewhat adequate expression for what is slowly coming into view inevitably have all kinds of prior linguistic associations that warp and falsify that view.

One might be inclined, for example, to see the idea of a series of levels in the changing viewpoint people have of themselves and their world as the extravagant product of a speculative fantasy. Or one may suspect it of implying the notion of an automatic, predetermined development, a necessary historical sequence, a self-evident improvement and progress, an unfolding of some supra-individual spirit; or of harbouring the idea – normally referred to by terms like "relativism" or "historicism" – that with the opening of a new perspective on consciousness everything that people have previously experienced, thought and said must become false and insignificant.

Nothing of the kind is true. The idea that what we reifyingly call "consciousness" is multi-layered is the outcome of an attempt to set up a new mental framework within which specific observations can be processed and that can serve as a guide for further observations. It is open to and in need of verification and revision in the light of further empirical research. That it has a Hegelian flavour really only proves that Hegel was in some respects on the track of phenomena that are open to empirical verification, even if he himself wove them into the structure of his speculative system to the point where it is difficult to disentangle what is capable of verification by other people from what is simply his personal metaphysics, as well as a justification of the social order in which he lived. Perhaps this intermingling actually put others off the track he had discovered.

The direction of this track can perhaps be most simply indicated by referring to an elementary feature of human experience: people are in a position to know that they know; they are able to think about their own thinking and to observe themselves observing. Under certain circumstances they can climb further and become aware of themselves as knowing that they are aware of themselves knowing. In other words, they are able to climb the spiral staircase of consciousness from one floor with its specific view to a higher floor with its view and, looking down, to see themselves standing at the same time on other levels of the staircase. Moreover, the perspective characteristic of these other levels is assimilated into their own in one form or another, although its characteristics are not the same for people who take it for granted as for those who are able to view it with a certain detachment from a higher level of consciousness. How far up or down one climbs this staircase depends not only on the talent, personality structure or intelligence of individual people, but on the state of development and the total situation of the society to which they belong. They provide the framework, with its limits and possibilities, while the people either take advantage of the possibilities or let them lie fallow.

V

What happened in Descartes's time was a transition to a new level of self-consciousness. The difficulties that he and some of his contemporaries and successors encountered arose to a large extent because people were unable to reconcile the characteristics they observed in themselves on the spiral staircase when viewing themselves as the subjects of knowledge and thought, and the different characteristics they found when they saw themselves simply as the objects of human thought and observation.

They took the different views they had of themselves as knowers and known to be different components of themselves.

Thus Descartes's reflections, for example, express the experience of a person who on one hand began to perceive himself as a thinker and observer independent of authorities and reliant only on himself in his thinking, and on the other as part of what he observed, a body among others. But with the means of reflection available to him at that time it was difficult to attain a proper conceptual understanding of this double role as observer and observed, knower and known, subject and object of thought and perception. In one way or another the two roles presented themselves as different modes of being or even as separate entities. Or concepts were used in speech and thought that seemed to refer to different and perhaps quite separate things. And this tendency to speak and think about conceptually distinct, if indissolubly connected roles and functions as if they were separate entities, was typical of a whole age. One might say that a first, theologically and religiously orientated age, the Middle Ages, was followed by a second, metaphysically orientated one, in the thought and speech of which reified functions and feelings played a primordial role. This is one example.

As an observer the individual person confronted the world as a fairly free and detached being; he distanced himself to a certain extent from the world of inanimate things as from that of human beings, and therefore of himself. In his capacity as the observed, the human being perceived himself as part of a natural process and, in keeping with the state reached by thought in Descartes's time, as a part of the world of physical phenomena. This was viewed as a kind of clockwork mechanism or machine which, like other things of the same kind, was perceived through the senses. Accordingly, Descartes in his intellectual experiment posited his own existence in his capacity as a body as something that was just as uncertain, just as exposed to radical doubt, as all the other objects that we know through the mediation of the senses. The only thing he saw as indubitably existing was himself in his capacity as thinker and doubter. He observed and experienced himself on one hand in the way he was perceived by others, as if through their sense organs, or by himself in a mirror; and on the other hand, at the same time, he perceived himself in a manner which, he assumed, did not involve the mediation of the senses, i.e. as thinker and observer, the subject of experience. And like many other people who climbed to this level of self-consciousness, who observed themselves as observers, knew themselves as knowers, thought of and experienced themselves as thinkers and experiencers, he attributed each of the different ways in which he perceived himself to a different and separate plane of existence.

It was this type of dualism, of positing two views of oneself as separate and absolute, which for a long time determined the kinds of questions posed by epistemology – the more so because this same dualism increasingly formed the basic pattern of self-consciousness among the general population in most western societies. Such a step on the way to a new form of self-consciousness was certainly not unique. The Bible describes a step of the same kind. In paradise the ancestors of mankind were unaware of their nakedness; then they ate the forbidden fruit of knowledge and became aware of their nakedness. We find here a vivid expression of how closely the increase in self-consciousness is bound up with an increase of conscience.

What became perceptible in Descartes's age was a movement in the same direction, on a higher level of the spiral staircase. If people on the preceding level of self-consciousness had perceived themselves, in keeping with their education and mode of life, as members of associations such as family groups or estates embedded in a spiritual realm ruled by God, they now increasingly perceived themselves as individuals, though without entirely losing the old conception. The changed social modes of life imposed a growing restraint on feelings, a greater need to observe and think before one acted, with regard to both physical objects and human beings. This gave greater value and emphasis to consciousness of oneself as an individual detached from all other people and things. The act of detachment in observing others and oneself was consolidated into a permanent attitude and, thus fixed, generated in the observer an idea of himself as a detached being who existed independently of all others. The act of detachment when observing and thinking condensed into the idea of a universal detachment of the individual; and the function of experience, of thinking and observing, which can be perceived from a higher level of self-consciousness as a function of the *whole* human being, first presented itself in reified form as a component of the human being like the heart, stomach or brain, a kind of insubstantial substance *in* the human being, while the act of thinking condensed into the idea of an "intelligence", a "reason" or, in the antiquated term, a "spirit". The two aspects of the dout role that people have in relation to themselves and to the world at large – as knowers of themselves and as known by themselves, as experiencing themselves and others and as experienced by themselves and others, as detaching themselves from the world in contemplation and as indissolubly enmeshed in the events of the world – these two aspects were so hypostatized in the habits of thought and speech that they appeared to be different objects, such as "body" and "mind", one of which was housed inside the other like the stone in a plum. Indeed, the tendency to picture functions as substances went so far that the relation between them was conceived in spatial terms. The activity of observing and thinking peculiar to man and the accompanying retardation of action, the growing restraint of emotional impulses and the associated sense of being detached from and opposite to the world, was reified in consciousness as the idea of something that could be located inside human beings, just as they appeared as bodies among bodies in their capacity as observable objects of thought.

VI

The basic problem of epistemology corresponded to this form of human self-consciousness. It took its starting point from the absolute status conferred on the temporary self-detachment that is a part of the act of cognition at what we call the "scientific" stage of development. It was based on the notion of a knowing subject which stands opposed to the world of knowable objects, from which it is separated by a broad divide. The problem was how the subject was to gain certain knowledge of objects across this divide. The answers varied. But whether they took an empirical, rationalist, sensualist or positivist form, the basic structure of the question remained the same for centuries, up to our own day. It was one of the axiomatic truths of the period. One needs only to select a few examples from the multitude of classical theories of knowledge to see its special nature more clearly, and also the insoluble problems in which people constantly found themselves entangled as a result of this image of man, with its reification of specific human functions.

This was the basic position – always the same one. The self-perception of the person as observer and thinker was reified in speech and thought, giving rise to a notion of an entity within the human being which was cut off from everything going on outside itself by the walls of its bodily container, and which could gain information about outside events only through the windows of the body, the sense organs. How reliable this information was, whether the senses presented a distorted picture of what went on "outside", whether, indeed, there was anything "outside", whether and how far the "thinking thing" inside us, the *res cogitans* as Descartes called it, influenced and changed what came to us through the senses in its own way – all these were questions that had to be discussed over and over again, given the presuppositions that have been described.

A number of philosophers, first and foremost Berkeley, saw no way of convincing themselves that anything could exist independently of one's own perceptions. The statement "there is", Berkeley maintained, really means nothing other than "I perceive something". It does not imply that anything is happening outside myself, only that something is happening in me. My senses are excited, that is all. And it seemed to him that the only guarantee available to the "self" in its container that anything lasting existed outside it and corresponded in some way to its conceptions, was God.

That was certainly an extreme position in the epistemological controversy. But perhaps because it is extreme it shows up the image of man common to all the contending positions particularly clearly. Other philosophers no doubt showed greater confidence in the reliability of our senses. They assumed that eyes and ears give us a fairly faithful picture of the outer world. We receive sense impressions from the things outside us, they thought, and distil from them simple conceptions of certain qualities of things, such as the ideas of colour, form, size and solid mass. That was the position adopted by Locke, for example. But even the exponents of this standpoint came up against certain characteristic difficulties. They might say: "I can perceive something which is green, rectangular, solid and heavy. But how do I know that all these qualities are related to each other as qualities of one and the same thing? Everything the senses convey to me is information on certain qualities. Objects as such cannot be perceived with the senses. The question is therefore how I arrive at the more complex idea of a unified substrate for a collection of sense impressions." And at this point Locke, like many others who attempted to derive their conceptions of things and their relations from their own experience, found himself and his arguments in considerable difficulty. Starting from the basic pattern, accepted as self-evident even by his fiercest opponents, of an image of man comprising an "inside" and an "outside" with sense-impressions as the only bridge between them, Locke adopted the position that consciousness, reason or whatever else the insubstantial inner thing might be called, gradually filled with knowledge derived from sense-impressions like an initially empty vessel. The difficulty was how to explain, from this standpoint, how a person can arrive at a conception of relationships, particularly regular and necessary relationships, between individual sense-impressions or what gave rise to them. Where does one find concepts for relationships such as like and unlike, whole and part, cause and effect?

A number of philosophers following in Plato's footsteps offered an answer to questions of this kind which was simple enough in its approach. Concepts and ideas of this sort, they argued, could not be imprints made inside us by material objects outside us. They were part of the natural equipment of our reason or our soul. Some exponents of this line of argument put more stress on the divine origin of such ideas while others considered them an innate part of human nature. But, of course, it was still open to question how far people could experience things "outside" them through the veil of these pre-existing ideas, what they were like independently of the person experiencing them – unless, like Leibniz, one sought a way out of the dilemma by assuming a pre-stabilized harmony between "inside" and "outside". Whatever these pacifying hypotheses might be, on the other side were the sceptics who declared that nothing of the kind could be demonstrated. In many cases it was probably only the pressure of public opinion or the power of church and state that prevented them from saying openly that all these ideas were comforting daydreams in the guise of reason. David Hume, for example, with his incorruptible intellectual integrity, contented himself with noting – very logically in relation to his presuppositions – that he could find no reason for asserting a necessary relation between individual sense impressions. As far as he could see, such ideas were probably based on the repetition of experiences, on habit or habituation. And Kant, who applied the extraordinary acuity and fertility of his mind to an attempt to produce a synthesis of these antinomies, found himself no less deeply embroiled in the labyrinth of insoluble problems generated by the common assumptions underlying this philosophical dispute. He imagined that in our knowledge of the world experiences coming to us from outside through the senses merged with forms of relations and ideas present in our consciousness prior to all experience. And even if his contribution represented a considerable refinement of the notion of the innate ideas, the elementary difficulties in which they became caught up were the same. In the end he too found himself confronted by the question whether one could really know things in themselves, as they were independently of the pre-existing forms of consciousness, or whether these primal ideas and forms of relationship which existed a priori and which, he assumed, were the eternal and unalterable appurtenances of human consciousness, condemned human beings for ever to perceive objects as they appear as a result of these appurtenances.

There we have the problem. The protracted argument about knowledge revolved basically around this question: are the signals received by the individual through his senses related together and processed by a kind of innate mechanism called "intelligence" or "reason" according to mental laws which are common to all people, eternal, existing prior to experience? Or do the ideas the individual forms on the basis of these signals simply reflect things and people as they are independently of his ideas? There were intermediate positions, compromises, syntheses, but they all lay somewhere on the continuum between these two poles.

And this common basic schema underlying the questions was closley bound up with another common schema concerning self-consciousness and the image of man, and with basic ideas about the self and its relation to the non-self which thinkers accepted without question.

VII

The unquestioned image of man underlying this philosophical dispute was undoubtedly different from the one that played a part in the preceding argument among the great scholastic philosophers. But it was also a continuation of it. In a more or less secularized form, and conceived now in relation to and now in isolation from God, it showed its descent from an ecclesiastical ancestor. The idea of a duality of body and soul had previously provided people with an intellectual framework for understanding themselves and now lived on in a special enclave, in conjunction with other-wordly questions concerning invisible, unobservable relationships such as the destiny of people and things. It was now changed, in conjunction with this-worldy questions about the nature of our knowledge of visible, observable objects, into the idea of a duality of body and mind, reason, consciousness, or whatever it may be called.

"I am a person," this basic schema might run in a simple form, "and I have a body. My body is made of matter, has spatial extent and therefore a certain position in space. But my reason, my mind, consciousness or self is not made of matter nor does it extend in space. Reason and intelligence, mind and consciousness have their seat *in* my body, but are different *from* my body." And it was this strange notion of an un-thinglike thing which, though not spatial, occupies a very definite position in space, inside my body, the idea that "I" or "my intelligence", "my consciousness", "my mind" is contained in my body as in a diving suit, that provided the common basis even to diametrically opposed views in the epistemological controversy. As the unquestioned framework of self-perception it underlay the question whether and how far the ideas "within" corresponded to the objects "outside". That is the core of the matter. People experienced themselves as closed systems.

Moreover, the "subject of knowledge", called by the most diverse names in the various theories of knowledge, corresponded to this idea. The model underlying it was an individual "I" in its container. Everything that was "outside", whether thing or human being, approached it as if after the event, as something unknown and strange which stood alone in face of the world, like the philosopher, as an observer and thinker seeking an answer to a question. Even if the idea of other people was included in one's arguments, they were seen essentially as a collection of closed systems each of which, exactly as one seemed to do oneself, looked from "inside" at a world lying "outside". In keeping with the basic pattern of self-perception they were not seen as something to which one could say "you" or "we", but, so to speak, as a mass of "I's". And this "I" of knowledge, the *homo philosophicus* of classical epistemology, was, on close inspection, a grown-up who had never been a child. The question was how a "rational" person, a person with the mental apparatus of an adult, could gain knowledge of the world. For the purpose of epistemology one abstracted from the observation that every adult was once a child; it was set aside as irrelevant to the problem of how knowledge was acquired. The question was how a rational, adult individual could here and now gain knowledge of things "outside". The concept of development was hardly available, as a means of thinking about society, to the schools of philosophy engaged in the epistemological controversy up to about the beginning of the nineteenth century, or only in a primitive form. It was a concept of relationships that had not yet properly developed.

Hume, who never allowed himself to shrink back from any conclusion to which the logic of his ideas led him, expressed this quite unequivocally in his fundamental position. It is not a little instructive, even for understanding one's own thought, to see him wrestling vainly with a problem which is often answered today without further reflection by using the commonplace concept of development – at least in everyday life. On a more technical level there are still many unsolved problems attached to the concept.

A person, Hume said to himself, was once a child and is now a man. He has changed in every respect, even physically. What, therefore, is the likeness or identity between the child and the man? What do we mean when we say he is the same person? The usual answer is: Whatever the changes he has undergone, his different parts are connected together by a causal relationship. But Hume found this answer highly unsatisfactory. The idea of an identical substrate seemed to him suspect even when applied to inanimate objects. It seemed much more suspect when applied to human beings. As he could never convince himself that words like "cause" and "effect" referred to a relationship subject to regularity or law, as he could not understand why a causal connection was anything other than a relationship that could be frequently observed, the talk of an identity between child and man seemed to him fundamentally fictitious. It is, he wrote, of the same kind as that which we ascribe to plants and animal bodies. Most philosophers seem inclined to assume that personal identity springs from consciousness. But consciousness, as he saw it, is nothing but a collection of ideas and sense perceptions. "I can discover no theory which appears to me fitting and satisfactory on this point." Here too Hume was following his train of thought to its extreme conclusion. Unlike other metaphysicians, who generally found unanswered questions intolerable, he was able to look it straight in the face and say: "I do not know the answer." But the basic structure of the image of man which gave rise to the question was, as we see, always the same.

The point can perhaps be more easily grasped with the help of a parable – the parable of the thinking statues. On the bank of a broad river, or perhaps on the steep slope of a high mountain, stands a row of statues. They cannot move their limbs. But they have eyes and can see. Perhaps ears as well, that can hear. And they can think. They have "understanding". We can assume that they do not see each other, even though they well know that others exist. Each stands in isolation. Each statue in isolation perceives that something is happening on the other side of the river, or the valley. Each forms ideas of what is happening, and broods on the question how far these ideas correspond to what is happening. Some think that such ideas simply mirror the happenings on the other side. Others think that much is contributed by their own understanding; in the end one cannot know what is going on over there. Each statue forms its own opinion. Everything it knows comes from its own experience. It has always been as it is now. It does not change. It sees. It observes. Something is happening on the other side. It thinks about it. But whether what it thinks corresponds to what is going on over there remains unresolved. It has no way of convincing itself. It is immobile. And alone. The abyss is too deep. The gap is unbridgeable.

VIII

The type of human consciousness this parable refers to is certainly not only a thing of the past. The individual's feeling of being ultimately alone which it expresses, the feeling of standing in isolation, opposed to the "outside world" of people and things, and of being "inwardly" something forever separated from what exists "outside", may be even more universally taken for granted in many western societies today than it ever was in the past, even in the age of the classical European philosophers a few centuries ago. It has struck deep roots in the languages which are implanted in young people as tools of understanding in these societies, roots so deep that it is almost impossible, in speaking and thinking about the functioning and behaviour of human beings, to avoid reifying spatial analogies like "inner life" and "outer world", "seat of reason", "contents of consciousness", "his reason ought to tell him that . . .", "he knows inside himself . . .". They usually impose themselves on thought as quite self-evident. We hardly realize that in using such expressions we ascribe to certain human activities spatial qualities which, like other functions and activities of human beings, they do not in reality possess. It makes sense to say that the heart and lungs are situated inside the chest cavity. One can locate the brain inside the cranium and certain brain functions in the brain itself. But it makes no proper sense to say that something takes place *inside* these functions, inside consciousness or thought. One cannot really say that something takes place inside speaking or outside walking. Equally, there is little point in saying that consciousness has its seat in the brain or reason its seat inside the human being. One does not, after all, say that speech has its seat in the throat and mouth, or walking in the legs.

The parable of the thinking statues gives us an indication why the idea that consciousness, feeling, understanding or even the actual "self" is located "inside" the human being, seems so convincing, at least to people in certain social groups. It suggests that we are dealing with the self-perception of people on whose behaviour a relatively high degree of restraint has been imposed by the nature of social life and the corresponding mode of bringing up children. Behaviour control of one sort or another no doubt exists in all human societies. But here, in many western societies, such control has for several centuries been particularly intensive, complex and pervasive; and more than ever before social control is linked to the self-control of the individual. In children instinctual, emotional and mental impulses and the muscular movements, the behaviour towards which they impel the child, are still completely unseparated. As they feel, so they must act. As they speak, so they think. As they grow up the elementary, spontaneous impulses on one hand and the motorial discharge, the actions and behaviour following from them on the other are separated more and more. Countervailing impulses formed on the basis of individual experiences intervene between them. And as the basic pattern of these experiences differs in different societies, the basic pattern of this self-control and its whole relation to the elementary, spontaneous impulses common to all people differs in different societies. This intervention of contrary impulses between the spontaneous, universal human impulses and the discharge in action has, over several centuries in European societies – for reasons we need not go into here – become especially deep, uniform and comprehensive. A finely woven net of controls fairly evenly encompassing not just some but all areas of human existence is, in one form or another, sometimes in contrary forms, instilled like a kind of immunization into young people by the example, the words and actions of the adults. And what was first a social command finally becomes, mainly through the mediation of parents and teachers, second nature to the individual, in accordance with his or her particular experiences. "Don't touch it", "Sit still", "Don't eat with your fingers", "Where's your handkerchief?", "Don't make yourself dirty", "Stop hitting him", "Do as you would be done by", "Can't you wait?", "Do your sums", "You'll never get any-where", "Work, work, work", "Think before you act", "Think of your family", "Think about the future", "Think of the Party", "Think of the church", "Think of England", or "Germany, Russia, India, America", "Think on God", "Aren't you ashamed?", "Have you no principles?", "You have no conscience".

The direct discharge of impulses in activity or even movement grows more and more difficult. Diverse and often highly complex detours for such tendencies – away from the discharge they spontaneously seek – become the rule. To react precipitously, without lengthy trial actions, the silent anticipation of future chess-moves that we call "reflection", is hardly possible for adults in such societies. Often enough it is dangerous, punishable or invites ostracism; and for the one who loses control the threat from others is often less strong than the threat from himself – through fear, shame or conscience. The time-lag between the thought, the trial actions rehearsed without any movement, and the actuation of the limbs in the act itself grows longer and longer. Leaving aside a few situations which are socially clearly defined, the socially instilled control-impulses, reified by terms such as "understanding", "reason" or "conscience", usually block the direct access of other, more spontaneous impulses, whether of instinct, feeling or thought, to motorial discharge in action. The feelings, the self-perception of the individual which present themselves in thought and speech as an encapsulation of his "inside" from the world "outside", from other things and people, are very closely bound up with this growth of individual self-control in the course of a specific social development. What is expressed in it is the deflection of spontaneous tendencies away from direct discharge in action by the interposing of the stricter and more complex control functions of the individual himself.

Where love and hate can be easily and spontaneously discharged in action, the communal life of people, unless secured by powerful social organs of control, is highly volatile. People come easily and frequently into contact with each other and make heavy emotional demands on each other, demands that are satisfied or unsatisfied, that bring joy or sorrow. Where such impulses are only able to express themselves in action in a muted, delayed, indirect manner, with strong habitual self-control, the individual is often overcome by the feeling of being cut off from all other people and the entire world by an invisible barrier. And in keeping with the logic of emotive thought, in which things that are objectively irreconcilable can easily appear reconcilable and identical if they are imbued with the same feeling, this invisible barrier is often felt to merge with the visible body. The body, as it appears to feeling, separates person from person like a wall, even if one is well aware that it is also what unites them. It seems like a container that cuts one off from the "outside" and "contains" one's own person or, as the case may be, "consciousness", "feeling", "reason" and "conscience", like a receptable.

Transformations of consciousness of this kind are both *historical*, in that whole societies have undergone or are still undergoing them today, and *personal*, in that every child undergoes them in growing up. As they proceed, more and more activities that originally engaged the whole person with all his limbs, are concentrated on the eyes, although, of course, excessive restriction of this kind can be compensated by activities such as dance or sport. With the increasing suppression of bodily movements the importance of seeing grows: "You can look at that but don't touch it", "Nice figure", "Not too close, please". Or the same can happen with speech: "You can call someone names, but not hit them", "Sticks and stones may break my bones but names can never hurt me", "Keep your hands off me". Pleasures of the eyes and ears become richer, more intense, subtler and more general. Pleasures of the limbs are hemmed in more and more to a few areas of life. One perceives much and moves little. One thinks and observes without stirring from the spot. The parable of the thinking statues exaggerates, but it achieves the effect it is supposed to. The statues see the world and form conceptions of the world, but they are denied movement of their limbs. They are made of marble. Their eyes see, and they can think about what they see, but they cannot go up to it. Their legs cannot walk, their hands grasp. They look from outside into a world or from inside out into a world – however one chooses to put it – a world which is always separate from them.

The feeling of such a void or, to use the other image, of an invisible wall between person and person, self and world, is expressed very frequently, directly or indirectly, in the recent history of the West. It may be completely authentic, but quite often it hangs like a veil across the idea we have of the relationship between the human being in search of knowledge and the object of his knowledge, giving it, as we have seen, a quality of fantasy. It also gives a misleading twist to our ideas on the relation of person to person, individual to society. And it is by no means the universal human feeling it often appears to be to introspection. It is a symptom of the situation and the particular make-up of people in specific societies. One might suppose that it might be of some value to the practical task of communicating with members of different societies to divest this experience and the images of man associated with it of their self-evident quality. If one were to sum it up in the reifying language we are accustomed to, one might say that it is, above all, a specific form of conscience that is responsible for the feeling of an invisible wall between the "inner" and "outer" worlds, between individual and individual, "self" and "world".

In the metaphysical philosophies of the present, particularly in a number of existentialist writings, the problem of the invisible wall is expressed in the very choice of questions to be discussed. The writers concentrate on problems affecting the individual alone, such as solitude, *Angst*, pain and death. And as the exponents of contemporary metaphysics usually dismiss questions of perception and knowledge from the centre of interest, concentrating instead on problems of human "existence" as such, or of "immediate experience", one can often see more clearly what distinguishes their concerns from those of the classical European philosophers of the seventeenth and eighteenth centuries than what they have in common with them. But the great classical philosophers were certainly not concerned exclusively with questions of "reason", as is often alleged – a reason sometimes characterized rather condescendingly, though with a considerable use of rational argument, as "dry" or "arid". In their way they, like their recent successors, sought an answer to questions concerning the place of man in the world, or his relation to other people. And in this respect their approach hardly differed from that of the metaphysical philosophers of the present. With very few exceptions, both were primarily concerned with questions of *the* human being, as if the existence of a plurality of people, the problem of the co-existence of human beings, was something added accidentally and extraneously to the problems of the individual person. Problems such as aloneness or "direct experience", and that of knowledge, in which an isolated "subject" stands opposed to the world of "objects" in his search for certainty, are closely related. The unquestioned image of man and the notion of self-perception underlying it is essentially the same in both cases. The philosopher, if his ideas do not lose themselves in nebulous notions of supra-individual existence, takes up his position "in" the single individual. He looks through his eyes at the world "outside" as if through small windows; or he meditates from the same standpoint on what is happening "within".

Individualization in the Social Process

I

Philosophers are certainly not the only members of their societies and their age who perceive themselves, other people and the world at large in the manner we have described. We have chosen some of their *leitmotivs* as examples since they make available in more articulate and tangible form a manner of perceiving oneself and one's fellow human beings that is widespread in these societies without always finding such clear expression.

To summarize what has been said, they are characteristic of an age in which more and more functions to do with the protection and control of the individual that were previously exercised by small groups like the tribe, or the parish, manor, guild or estate, are being transferred to highly centralized and increasingly urbanized states. As this transfer proceeds, individual people, once they are grown up, increasingly leave behind the close, local protective groups based on blood. The groups' cohesion breaks down as they lose their protective and control functions. And within the larger, centralized and urbanized state societies the individual must fend far more for himself. The mobility of people, in the spatial and social sense, increases. Their involvement, previously inescapable throughout life, in family, kin group, local community and other such groups, is reduced. They have less need to adapt their behaviour, goals and ideals to the life of such groups or to identify themselves automatically with them. They depend less on them for physical protection, sustenance, employment, for the protection of inherited or acquired property or for help, advice and sharing in decisions. This happens first in limited special groups but extends gradually in the course of centuries to broader sections of the population, even in rural areas. And as individuals leave behind the closely knit, pre-state groups within the more and more complex state societies, they find themselves confronted with an increasing number of choices. They can decide far more for themselves. But they also *must* decide far more for themselves. They not only *can* but *must* be more self-sufficient. On this point they have no choice.

The possibility, like the necessity, of greater individualization is an aspect of a social transformation which is quite beyond the control of the individual. The product of this increasing individuality, the greater diversity of individual people with regard to behaviour, experience and make-up, is not simply given by nature in the same sense as is the diversity of human bodies. Nor is the separateness of individuals that is sometimes talked about a phenomenon given by nature in the same sense as the separateness of individual people in space. Considered as bodies, the individuals embedded for life in tightly knit kinship communities were and are no less separate from each other than the members of complex state societies. What emerges far more in the latter is the separateness and encapsulation of individuals *in their relations to each other*.

These relations, the whole manner of their social co-existence, lead increasingly to a general control of affects, to the denial and transformation of instincts. As this social change proceeds people are prevailed upon more and more to hide from each other or even from themselves bodily functions or instinctual manifestations and desires that were earlier either given free expression or were only held in check by fear of other people, so that they became normally unconscious of them.

What presents itself from one aspect as a process of increasing individualization is from another a process of civilization. It can be taken as characteristic of a certain phase of this process that tensions between the social commands and prohibitions that are internalized as self-control, and the suppressed spontaneous impulses, intensify. It is, as we have said, this conflict within the individual, this "privatization", the exclusion of certain spheres of life from social intercourse and the association with them of socially instilled anxiety, such as feelings of shame or embarrassment, which arouses within the individual the feeling that he is "inwardly" something quite separate, that he exists without relation to other people, only relating "retrospectively" to those "outside" him or her. On close examination this mode of self-perception is seen to stand the process which led up to it on its head. True and genuine as it may be as an expression of the peculiar personality structure of the individual at a certain stage of the movement of civilization, at the same time it stands in the way of an unprejudiced manner of observing the relations of person to person. The gap and the conflict between the more spontaneous impulses and the impulses which curb immediate action which are felt by the highly individualized people at this stage of civilization, are projected by them on to their world. They often appear in their theoretical reflections as an existential void between one human being and another, or as the eternal clash between individual and society.

II

We should also consider that in societies at this stage the adaptation of young people to their adult functions usually happens in a way which particularly reinforces such tensions and splits within the personality. The more complex and all-embracing the self-restraint, the more intense and many-sided the instinct-control demanded by the correct performance of the roles and functions of adults in a society, the greater become the divergence between the behaviour of children and that of adults. The remodelling of the individual in growing up, the individual civilizing process in the course of which he moves from the starting point of infantile behaviour, which is everywhere the same, to a greater or lesser approximation to the standard of civilization attained by his society, becomes more difficult and takes longer. The time-span needed to prepare young people for the more complex roles and functions of an adult lengthens.

As the gap between the spontaneous behaviour of children and the attitude demanded of an adult increases, it becomes less and less possible to place the child at an early age, as is done in simpler societies, on the bottom rung of the functional ladder the top of which he is intended to reach. Even in the society of the European Middle Ages the young person was often trained in the direct service of an adult master. The page serves the knight, the apprentice the guildmaster. And even if the period of service was long and the top rung unattainable to the individual in many cases, the career-ladder itself was relatively short and had few rungs. When societies become more complex and more centralized, when specialization increases and the careers offered by society lengthen, the preparation needed for the performance of adult tasks also grows longer and more complex. For a long and still lengthening period children and young people are isolated from adult circles: they go to school, study at universities, technical colleges and other institutions specially organized for the preparation of young people. The number and the specialization of such institutes increase, and access to them broadens. As adult professions become more and more specialized and complex young people from wider and wider sections of the population undergo an indirect preparation in special institutes of one kind or another instead of the direct preparation prevalent earlier. Adult life-expectancy increases. So too does the time of preparation for adulthood. Biologically mature people remain socially immature. They are boys and girls, teenagers, callow youth or whatever they may be called, no longer children and not yet men and women. They lead a separate social existence, having a "youth culture" – a world of their own which diverges strikingly from that of adults. And while the lengthening and the indirectness of their preparation, caused by the constant expansion of knowledge, may facilitate their assimilation to adult social life, emotionally it often makes it more difficult.

The professional tasks open to the mass of individuals on the long road of industrialization and urbanization within the tension-laden societies of transition, coincide only in a minority of cases with the expectations of the young. Specialized as they are, in most cases they allow limited scope to the inclinations and faculties of individuals. There is often no proper congruence or continuity between life in the reserve of youth and the mostly restricted fields of adult activity. In these complex societies the former are like special enclaves or islands from which no straight path leads to the latter. The transition from one sphere to the other is not uncommonly marked by a noticeable caesura in the life of the individual, that he or she accommodates with greater or lesser difficulty. In passing through these enclaves the young person can and must experiment frequently, either with new experiences, or with others in relation to himself and himself in relation to others. The scope for experimentation that is open to him bears no relationship to the relative constriction, uniformity and regularity of the life which in many cases awaits the adult. In the social life of this age-group abilities and interests are often developed for which adult functions within this structure allow no scope; forms of behaviour and inclinations that adults must restrain or suppress.

With the growing specialization of societies the individual's path on the way to becoming a self-reliant, self-determining person grows longer and more complicated. The demands on his or her conscious and unconscious self-control increase. An additional factor which impedes the young person's assimilation to adult society is the lengthening of and the special form taken by the period between childhood and social adulthood. This also increases the probability that the person in question will not be able to attain a proper balance between personal inclinations, his own self-control and his social duties.

III

The basic pattern of the image of the self, and of man in general, thus continues to be based, even in the most advanced types of social specialization and individualization that have emerged so far, on the idea of an "inside" which is separated from the world "outside" as if by an invisible wall. But in the idea of the outer world natural events no longer play the same part as they did in the seventeenth or eighteenth centuries, for example. The antithesis between individual and nature, beween the knowledge-seeking subject and the natural objects of knowledge, gradually loses its importance. It does not do so because the epistemological problems that present themselves in this form of reflection have found a convincing solution – that is hardly the case – but because these problems are clearly becoming less urgent as people become increasingly able to gain control of natural processes in thought and action and to use them for their own purposes. Physical processes in particular are visibly losing their character as mysterious, untameable and dangerous powers that frequently irrupt into the lives of people. In their place the members of these societies see themselves increasingly as the wielders of power who are able to decipher the puzzles of nature and to bend her processes to their own ends. And as the systematic investigation of natural powers, after long resistance, slowly becomes something commonplace, their exploitation for human purposes something taken for granted, natural objects no longer play the same part as before in the idea of the "outside world" which stands opposed to the "inside" of the human being, separated from it as by an invisible wall. It is as if people had said to themselves: "It may be that we cannot agree on whether and how far the ideas we have of natural events actually correspond to things in themselves, independent of human observation. But look at our power stations, our machines, our railways and aeroplanes. We can extract more food from our land and more milk from our cows. We are even slowly getting the better of disease. In practice, where thought and action connect, we are well able to establish a high degree of correspondence between our ideas and expectations of natural events and these events themselves. If philosophers are unable to explain theoretically how such an increasing congruence is possible, so much the worse for them – *tant pis pour les philosophes.*"

What can be actually observed is the following: with the increasing shift in the relations between human beings and extra-human natural forces, the latter slowly recede as an element within the notion of the "outer world" that stands opposed to the human "inner world". In their place the gulf between the "inner" part of the individual and other people, between the true inner self and "external" society, moves into the foreground. As natural processes become easier to control, it appears that our relative lack of control over the relations between people and particularly between groups, and the insuperable obstacles which social demands put in the way of personal inclinations, become all the more perceptible.

In this way the metaphysical symbol of growing individualization, the individual's idea that his inner self is cut off from a world out there as if by an invisible wall, is perpetuated. But it presents itself more as expressing one person's feeling of being cut off from others, or the "individual" 's feeling of being separated from "society", and less as expressing a gulf between man and nature. And the notion of this "inner" self that is cut off from the outer world is broadened. The change that can be observed in a number of metaphysical systems devised by philosophers has its counterpart in changes in the way more and more sections of society perceive themselves. In this perception the emphasis often shifts from "reason" as the distinctive feature of the "inner" self that is divorced from the "outer" world, to something that is really only a reification of the same thing on a broader basis, the "whole life", the "existence" of the human being. In this broader field of society we not infrequently come across self-images in which the idea of the inner self is based not only on intellectual functions but on feelings, on the "real nature" of the whole person and not least on the more animal aspects of human being, as these aspects become increasingly privatized.

Thus a person might express the feeling that social life denies fulfilment to his inner self. He may feel that society impels him to violate his "inner truth". The word "society" is often used in such contexts as if it referred to a person. Through such usage the word tends to take on the quality of a mother in her role as a cold, hostile, restrictive and oppressive force, denying the child satisfactions and forcing it to hold back within itself all that which it would like to do, show and express. In this, society is quite unlike "nature", as presented in the metaphysics of what we call the "modern period". Unlike its treatment in earlier ages, nature is seen more and more as a thoroughly friendly person who, though she may have her whims, is a symbol of everything good, healing, normal and healthy, in short, "natural". Thus, in the popular and even the scholarly metaphysics of the age, "society" is often presented as that which prevents individual people from enjoying a "natural" or "authentic" life. What one is within oneself, independently of other people, what one believes one's "inner self" to be, is associated with the emotive complex surrounding the word "nature". The inner self is perceived as "natural", while one's dealings with other people are regarded as something imposed from "outside", a mask or shell placed by "society" over the natural inner core. It is now "society" which stands opposed, as the "outer world", to the "inner self", unable, it might seem, to touch the "authentic, inner core". In a slight variation of this motif, society is seen as a gaoler forbidding the individual to step out of his or her inner cell.

"From my cell I look out into life," thus Rilke expresses it in one of his poems.[2] "From people I am further than from things; people are mere accidents, voices, fears, masks. No one lives his own life. Perhaps there are somewhere treasure-houses where all these unlived lives are stored like armour, cradles or garments that no one has ever used. All paths lead finally to this arsenal of unlived things. It is like a prison without windows. Doors with iron clasps and bars block the entrance. And the bars are made by human hands."

These lines, paraphrased here, give clear, exemplary expression to a form of human self-perception and suffering that is undoubtedly not restricted to poets and philosophers. In society at large this perception may not always be so clear or its expression so vivid. The intensity of such feelings varies from person to person. But the human situation that Rilke expresses in his own way here is a part of what would earlier have been called the *Zeitgeist*, the "spirit of the age". It is part of the basic configuration of people living in certain social groups. As both a social and an individual phenomenon, this kind of experience forms part of the general change in the course of which more and more people detach themselves from small, less differentiated, closely knit communities and spread in a movement like an unfolding fan to form the more complex societies and finally the nation states within which they keep a greater personal distance from each other.

In the earlier, closer communities the most important factor in controlling individual behaviour is the constant presence of others, the knowledge of being tied for life to others and not least the direct fear of others. The individual person has neither the opportunity, nor the need, nor the capacity to be alone. Individuals have hardly any opportunity, desire or ability to take decisions on their own or to think any thoughts without constant reference to the group. That does not mean that the members of such a group live harmoniously together. The opposite is often the case. It means only that – to use our catchword – they think and act primarily from the "we" standpoint. The make-up of the individual is attuned to constant co-existence with others to whom behaviour has to be adjusted.

In industrialized, heavily populated, urbanized societies adults have a far greater opportunity, as well as the need and the capacity, to be alone, or at least alone in pairs. To choose for oneself between the many alternatives is a necessity that soon becomes a habit, a need and an ideal. The control of behaviour by others is joined by increasing self-control in all spheres of life. And as is often the case, attributes of the human make-up that are rated positively on the social scale of values are structurally linked to others that are rated negatively. One such attribute on the positive side is the pride of highly individualized people in their independence, their freedom, their ability to act on their own responsibility and to decide for themselves. On the other hand we have their greater isolation from each other, their tendency to perceive themselves as having an inner self inaccessible to others, and the whole range of feelings associated with this perception, such as the feeling of not living one's own life, or the feeling of radical solitude. Both these are aspects of the same basic pattern or personality structure. But because they are given opposite valuations, because they each have a different emotive tone, we are inclined to see them as independent phenomena with no connection between them.

In other words, the development of society towards a higher level of individualization in its members opens the way to specific forms of fulfilment and specific forms of dissatisfaction, specific chances of happiness and contentment for individuals and specific forms of unhappiness and discomfort that are no less society-specific.

The opportunity individuals now have to seek the fulfilment of personal wishes on their own and largely on the basis of their own decisions, carries with it a particular kind of risk. It demands not only a considerable amount of persistence and foresight; it also constantly requires the individual to pass by momentary chances of happiness that present themselves in favour of long-term goals that promise more lasting satisfaction, or to juxtapose these to short-term impulses. Sometimes they can be reconciled, sometimes not. One can take a risk. One has the choice. More freedom of choice and more risk go together. One may reach the goals that give one's personal striving meaning and fulfilment, and so find the expected happiness. One may get halfway there. Perhaps the reality turns out less entrancing than the dream.

One may miss one's goal altogether and carry a sense of failure through life. War, upheaval and other social events may block the way. One may have misjudged the chances of reaching such goals from one's own social starting point. One may place too heavy demands on oneself; the goal which promises meaning and fulfilment may not best match one's aptitudes. The exertion of the long journey may be such that one loses the ability to enjoy the achievement or to see it as a proper fulfilment. One's ability to feel joy and fulfilment may have been stifled in childhood through family relationships. There are many such possibilities. The abundance of different individual opportunities and goals in such societies is matched by the abundant possibilities of failure.

The same is true of the "arsenal of unlived things". From a structural point of view, the wealth of missed opportunities matches the wealth of alternatives between which one can and must decide. Usually, one accepts what has been achieved without thinking back too much. But whether one remembers it or not, the path the individual has to tread in such complex societies – compared to the one open to the individual in less complex societies – is extraordinarily rich in branches and turnings, though not to the same degree, of course, for individuals from different social classes. It leads past a large number of forks and crossroads at which one has to decide whether to go this way or that. If one does look back it is easy to be beset by doubt. Should I not have taken a different turning? Didn't I neglect all the opportunities I had then? I have now attained this, I have produced this or that, have become a specialist in this or that, have I now let many other gifts wither? And put aside many things I might have done? It is in the nature of societies that demand a fairly high degree of specialization from their members that a large number of unused alternatives – lives the individual has not lived, roles he has not played, experiences he has not had, opportunities he has missed – are left by the wayside.

IV

In simpler societies there are fewer alternatives, fewer opportunities for choice, there is less knowledge about the connections between events and thus there are fewer opportunities that might appear in retrospect to have been "missed". In the simplest ones there is often only a single, straight path before people from childhood on – one path for women and another for men. Crossroads are rare, and seldom is a person placed alone before a decision. Here, too, life brings its risks with it, but the scope for choice is so small and exposure to the capricious power of natural forces so great that the risks hardly depend on decisions. They are mainly the risk everyone takes on coming into the world, the threat of physical destruction. And the preponderance of this risk is characteristic of both at once – of human nature and of the specific form of social life: the hunters may catch no prey; the people are in danger of starvation; and the weaker they get the less their chance of catching and eating their prey. Floods, roaring rivers and thundering clouds unexpectedly roll across the land and one cannot escape. Forest or brush fires block the way to safety. The sun beats down and the water-holes dry up. Animals, sickness or human foes attack and kill. The threat to life is omnipresent and commonplace. The spirits help or fly into a rage, no one knows why. One lives from day to day. One eats, one hungers, one dances, one dies. Any long-term view of something that might take place sometime in the future is very limited, far-sighted behaviour incomprehensible and undeveloped. No more comprehensible is the possibility of not doing something one feels urged to do here and now for the sake of a satisfaction that might come in a week or a year, or of doing what we call "work". Why should one make a muscular exertion without reference to the urgent demands of the moment?

This is the kind of social life that the ancestors of all the people living now led for far longer than the kinds of social life documented in written records during the short phase of human development that we call "history". Even the time when human groups began here and there to put the seeds of wild plants regularly and deliberately into the ground with a view to the nourishment they could expect months later, or to rear young animals in view of their future use, is hardly more than 10,000 years ago. Each major step on this path, whether it was the transformation of gatherer societies into settled agrarian ones, or hunters into cattle-raisers, whether the use of stones and bones as raw materials for tools and weapons gave way to that of metal, with all the secrets of its use that only specialists had access to, or whether centuries later manual industries changed into machine industries, in a certain respect the general direction of these and related changes was the same throughout the centuries.

Each of these changes presupposed and, in its turn, produced an increase in foresight. The interval between the first step towards a particular goal and the last, with which it is reached, grew longer and the intervening steps more numerous. It was short in the small groups in which adults could, and had to, perform all the activities necessary to satisfy their needs in the accepted social form, and in which they had all the necessary skills. These skills may have been in preparing stones and bones, gathering food, building winter protection or striking and making use of a spark from stone or wood. Gradually the interval grew longer. Implements became better suited to their uses; the number of special implements grew, as, no doubt, did the variety of skills. If the stone implements surviving from the early Stone Age are compared to those from the middle and late Stone Age, one has a good example of this increasing differentiation, although it developed incomparably more slowly than the differentiation and specialization of implements and skills in the industrial societies of the present. How long each individual adult possessed all the skills normal in that society during the 500,000 years – or it may have been 600,000 or 700,000 – in which stone of one kind or another served as the finest raw material for producing human implements, at what time specialists in particular skills began to emerge, is difficult to say. However that may be, in the course of time not only did the number of steps between the first and last in an action sequence multiply, but an increasing number of people were needed to perform these steps. And in the course of this process more and more people found themselves in growing dependence on each other, linked together as if by invisible chains. Each acted as a connecting link, a specialist with a limited task. Each was woven into a fabric of actions within which an increasing number of special functions, and of people with the skills to perform them, were interposed between the first step towards a social goal and the reaching of that goal.

And from a certain stage in the increasing division of functions, the number of special co-ordinating functions needed to maintain the interlocking of more and more specialized activities also began to grow. The longer the chains of actions grew, the more difficult it became for the individual woven into the network of dependence by his skills to gain an overall view; and the harder it became to distinguish what was the means and what the end.

In the history of a particular society shifts in this direction can be observed in different ways. One characteristic symptom of such a shift is the growing use of certain objects as generally recognized standards in transactions. Particular shells or even domestic animals can still have this function in dealings between groups that are loosely bound together. The use of pieces of metal the weight and social value of which are guaranteed by the stamp of a ruler or at least a central authority, implies a fairly solid organization. And the increase of money circulation in a society is a sure sign that the action chains in this society are taking on more links and that the division of functions is increasing, as is the formation of a state within that society.

When the ancestors of people living today, driven by hunger, picked up stones they found lying around and killed animals with them, they acted under the direct impulse of their present needs. When they sharpened stones even when they were not hungry to prepare for the coming hunt, or when they painted pictures of the animals on the ground and on rocks and killed their prey in the pictures even before it was present in reality, to be more sure of their food and to alleviate the general uncertainty of life, their foresight and the detour from the first step to the last were greater. But all this could still take place within the framework of small groups, who had to produce everything they needed themselves. And their ability to insert inhibiting, delaying or diverting control functions between the spontaneous instinctive impulse and the motorial performance of the act, their ability to oppose strong active urges successfully by mental acts, may not yet have been very great. Just as these people were more helplessly exposed to natural forces than their descendants, they were also more helpless in face of the natural forces within their own bodies.

Even when they had evolved biologically into what we call – none too modestly – *homo sapiens*, wise man, the species to which all the people alive now belong, we must assume that for a long time this was still the case. For the changes which followed – the advancing division of functions, the increase in foresight and the ability to curb short-term impulses, with all that these changes brought with them – were not symptoms of further bodily evolution but of a social and mental development in the same biological species. The body, arms and legs, eyes, ears and brain structure were already the same. But the cumulative experience of many hundreds of generations was needed before foresight, and the ability to restrain and control internal and external natural forces, grew continuously. And because the development in this direction was not a biological one, was not, as often seems to be believed, rooted in human nature, it can also be reversed. The long chains of actions with their division of functions can shrink again. The social and psychological control of behaviour can be reduced – not just here and there, as happens constantly at all times, but over the whole of humanity. And the specific kind of behaviour referred to by words like "civilized" or "individualized", can give way to forms of behaviour and experience driven by short-term animal impulses. And if we are able to restrain our own feeling that this or that is "better" or "desirable", and still more our fanciful notion that one or the other, "progress" or "decline and fall", is necessary and inevitable, it does not seem too difficult to ascertain under what conditions and for what reasons the movement goes one way or the other.

But however this may be, movements in both directions can always be observed in history, even if in the last millennia a particular movement has been predominant for long periods: the social and mental transformation of relatively small groups acting in a relatively short-term manner, with simple needs and uncertain fulfilment of these needs, into larger, more populous groups with a sharper division of functions, stronger control of behaviour, more complex and diverse needs and a more highly developed apparatus of co-ordination or government. The number of specialized activities which we call "professions" – not quite aptly, if this term implies a "calling" – has risen in the course of millennia, slowly at first, but now accelerating. To begin with it was probably just men and women who traditionally specialized in various activities and skills within the group, then perhaps magicians, warriors, farmers, shepherds or smiths. Or a whole tribe might develop a specialized skill at fishing and exchange its surplus catch in a fixed form for the fruit and edible roots of an inland tribe. Today many societies have hundreds of specialized occupations between which the individual has a degree of choice, depending on his or her social origin, schooling and talent. And the number of such occupations is growing more and more rapidly. We not only have doctors, but specialists for ears and eyes, for children and women, psychiatrists and specialists for internal diseases, and their number, like that of the auxiliary professions, increases constantly. We have not only engineers, but specialists in overground construction, shipbuilding, aeronautical engineering, power generation and a growing number of subdivisions. We not only have existing professions which are subdividing, but new professions which are coming into being.

But this is only the most recent phase of the long process. In its course the networks of separate functions in the chains of actions grew continuously longer and more complex. More and more people came to live in increasing dependence on each other, while each individual was at the same time growing more different from all others. The organizational units in which people were united grew larger and the organization itself more complex. Many small societies managed, and still manage, without permanent, specialized coordinating functions. The elders of a tribe might assemble and confer whenever it seemed necessary; otherwise they lived like all the rest. Someone might prove successful in hunts or war, and was followed. In the course of time, as village settlements changed here and there into urban settlements and city states as the division of functions advanced, and city states evolved into leagues of cities or kingdoms holding together several towns and the rural areas surrounding them in a looser or more centralized state organization, and dynastic states turned into nation states or world empires or federations of national states, whichever way the development went, there emerged not only official hierarchies, permanent specialized coordinating functions with a centre on a single level, but official hierarchies with their centres ranked vertically on many levels. The larger the area of land and the number of people and specialized activities within a state, the larger grew the number of superimposed levels in the government apparatus, and the variety of departments and offices.

As more and more people became dependent on each other as specialists of one kind or another within such a network of separate functions, it became increasingly necessary for their functions and activities to be harmonized. From this side too, the change in human relationships towards large, more centralized and specialized groups led to a greater restraint of momentary individual impulses. This may have been first imposed or maintained by the direct fear of others, overseers or the people nominated by the central ruler. But slowly the element of self-control in the harmonization of people to each other's activities became something more taken for granted. An increased use of clocks, to give only one example, is a sign of this. For whatever their importance as instruments for measuring non-human events, in their daily use by society they are primarily instruments for co-ordinating at a distance the activities of many people who are capable of a relatively high degree of self-control.

The direction of the changes therefore remained the same over very long periods, despite all the oscillations and backward movements that can be observed here and there. But within the framework of this movement there have been occasional break-throughs, that is, epochs when social and mental changes acting in the same direction have opened up new and previously un-imagined possibilities for life, and indeed for humanity itself. The conscious use of natural forces for human purposes, which seemed almost like something entirely new coinciding with the rise of science, was far more a continuation of efforts going back far into prehistory than is realized today. Although the mental approach to such efforts was different, the taming of fire, wild animals and plants for human use, like many other conquests of this kind, were steps in exactly the same direction as the exploita-tion of mineral oil or atomic energy for human purposes. Then too this extension of human control and knowledge usually led sooner or later to a specialization of human activities. Then as now the enlargement and specialization went hand in hand with an increased yield from work which, at first, for millennia benefited only restricted social groups, liberating only them from physical work to perform other functions.

Seen in this way, and there are many similar points, the more conscious and methodical control and use of natural processes by men on the basis of what we call "scientific research" was part of a slow and very gradual change in the relationship of human beings to non-human nature, to each other and, as individuals, to themselves. But at the same time it was a breakthrough to something new. We have already said that from now on, in the long struggle between man and non-human nature, the balance began to tilt, slowly at first but then faster and faster, towards man. Natural catastrophes could, of course, reverse this whole tendency. The potential preponderance of non-human nature over man is and remains overwhelming. But we can leave this larger perspective aside. As compared to earlier periods of human history, during the last phase the balance in the struggle with non-human forms of nature has shifted in favour of man.

From a social point of view this means not only that the division of functions accelerates, the interlocking specialized activities of people multiply and change; it means above all that the role of human muscle power which, with animal power, had probably been the main source of energy of human societies in the course of previous history, diminished visibly in the functioning of the specialized social structure. Broader and broader sections of society were liberated from physical, or at least from heavy physical work for activities in which skill, knowledge and education played an important part. Of course, people long knew how to make use of forms of inanimate energy available without human intervention, like wind or river currents. Now people began increasingly to make use of forms of energy which they were able to generate themselves with their own implements on the basis of methodical investigations. It was the growing use of physical energies like steam, electricity or nuclear energy, produced by social collaboration, which slowly and unevenly displaced the social use of human and animal muscle power.

Moreover, this change went hand in hand with a corresponding change in the social relationships between people, and within the individual person. The increasing control of non-human, natural forces by human beings was only possible, could only be sustained over a long period, within the framework of a stable, highly organized social structure. This stability and organization depended largely, in their turn, on the extensive control of natural forces. And, at the same time, the increasing control of natural forces was only possible in conjunction with increasing self-control by human beings. It could only be maintained with the aid of a fairly stable control of short-term affects and instincts, exerted partly by social institutions and partly by the individual himself. This latter kind of control could only develop and be maintained at a fairly high level in conjunction with an ordered management of social controls. Control of nature, social control and self-control form a kind of chain ring; they form a triangle of interconnected functions which can serve as a basic pattern for the observation of human affairs. One side cannot develop without the others; the extent and form of one depend on those of the others; and if one of them collapses, sooner or later the others follow.

V

We need to remember this long journey, in the course of which human societies gained increasing control of natural forces, in order to liberate ourselves from the rigid antitheses that frequently give rise to a short-sighted approach to human problems. Such control will undoubtedly be attained, if gradually, by all societies. It releases their members for many other tasks imposed by the protection of bare life, fear of the unknown and satisfaction of the most urgent needs in the immediate present. Antitheses like those between "nature" and "society", "individual" and "society", and the whole cluster of problems underlying the notion that something "inside" the individual, expressing his "nature", stands opposed to a social "outside world" which is not "natural" – all these have an appealing simplicity. They reflect valuations familiar to us, and for many people have a kind of felt truth that seems highly convincing. Nevertheless, they agree only slightly with the image of man that is gradually beginning to emerge from the careful work of many separate disciplines carried out over a long period, if their conclusions are viewed together. They not only veil and distort human problems themselves, obstructing a theoretical understanding of these problems; in many cases they also prevent effective action from being taken in relation to such problems. Instead of helping practical measures to solve them, they often have the opposite effect.

We need to recall this long developmental process of humanity above all in order to see the human characteristics referred to by terms such as "foresight", "intelligence", "civilization" or "individuality", not as something static and given for all time, but rather as something that is evolving and has evolved, as aspects of a process.

It is probably unusually difficult to realize today that qualities of human beings referred to by terms such as "individuality" are not simply given by nature, but are something that has developed from the biological raw material in the course of a social process. This is a process of "individualization", which in the great flow of human development is inseparable from other processes such as the increasing differentiation of social functions and the growing control of non-human natural forces.

Differences in behaviour, gifts and experience between individual people no doubt existed in the simplest human communities, still resembling those of animals, in prehistory. But the more people's actions are governed by untamed natural forces within themselves, the less they differ in their behaviour from each other. And the more diversely and pervasively these instinctive forces are restrained, diverted and transformed – first by love and fear of others, then also by self-control – the more numerous and pronounced become the differences in their behaviour, their feelings, their thoughts, their goals and not least their malleable physiognomies: the more "individualized" individuals become.

In the course of this process, not only do people become actually more different in their make-up, but the individual person becomes more aware of the difference. And from a certain stage of social development on, such differences take on a special value. With the increasing differentiation of society and the resulting individualization of individuals, this differentness of one person to all others becomes something that is ranked especially highly on the social scale of values. In such societies it becomes a personal ideal of young people and adults to differ from others in one way or another, to distinguish oneself – in short, to be different. Whether he realizes it or not, in such societies the individual is placed in a constant, partly tacit, partly explicit competitive struggle in which it is of utmost importance to his pride and self-respect that he can say to himself: "This is the quality, possession, achievement, gift by which I differ from the people I find around me, which distinguishes me from them." It is only another aspect of this human make-up and situation that expresses itself in the fact that, to a certain extent, the individual seeks meaning and fulfilment in something that only he does or is.

This ego-ideal of the individual, the desire to stand out from others, to stand on one's own feet and to seek fulfilment of a personal striving in one's own qualities, skills, possessions or achievements, is certainly a fundamental component of the individual person. It is something without which he would lose his identity in his own eyes as an individual. But it is not simply a part of his nature. It is something that has developed in him through social learning. Like other aspects of self-control or "conscience" it, emerges only gradually in history in this pronounced and pervasive form. It does so in conjunction with specific structural changes in social life. Even in the more complex societies of Europe, this ideal of being, having or accomplishing something unique and different, and the satisfaction its fulfilment brings, spreads only very gradually. It passes from small groups to large ones, at first more among men and far more slowly among women, who are usually drawn later into the competition between individuals, for special social reasons. Analogous changes in human beings and similar ideals can be observed at present in large areas of Africa and Asia, in conjunction with the formation of industrializing and urbanizing states – to begin with in relatively small groups and classes.

In other words, this ideal is part of a personality structure which only forms in conjunction with specific human situations, with societies having a particular structure. It is highly personal, yet at the same time society-specific. A person does not freely choose this ideal from a number of others, this being the one that appeals to him personally. It is the ideal of the individual person that is socially demanded and inculcated in the great majority of highly differentiated societies. Of course, one can oppose it even in such societies. There are retreats into which one can withdraw from the necessity of deciding for oneself and fulfilling oneself by standing out from others. But usually, for people brought up in such societies, this form of ego-ideal and the high degree of individualization corresponding to it, remain an integral part of their person, which they cannot be rid of, whether or not they approve of it.

Normally, people brought up in this way accept this form of striving and the behaviour that goes with it as self-evident and "natural". The personal ideal of individual fulfilment through actively aiming towards a goal which the individual regards as significant within his society, suits the specific situation in which the individual is placed in such societies. It puts him in a position to make use of the relatively wide scope for choice, the relatively high degree of freedom, that individuals are given in societies of this kind. At a young age he can and must select from the profusion of possible goals which such societies offer him, first through the position of his parents and then through the one he himself attains, this or that goal that promises the best fulfilment of his personal inclinations and aspirations. He can aim at professional or leisure activities that, he believes, will give him a chance to stand out from others, stand on his own feet and become independent, even from his parents or tribe; he can seek something that will set him apart from all his relations and acquaintances, allow him to achieve or become something especially outstanding, unique or "great" in the controlled competition of individuals. For that is what ranks highest in the scale of values of such societies, and assures the individual of respect, applause and often love.

But one can, of course, make mistakes. That is the risk I referred to earlier. For the chances of achieving the fulfilment of such a striving in such a society are always slight in relation to the number of people seeking it. It is difficult to estimate how great this discrepancy is in a particular society at a given time, although there are specific symptoms of its increasing or decreasing. But we can leave this problem aside. Whatever the case may be, the discrepancy itself can serve as an example of a problem which is of central importance in this context.

What we are concerned with here is not a discrepancy between a non-social, innate striving of the individual and a social structure which denies this striving fulfilment. Rather, it is a personal striving which is learned, produced by specific social institutions and experiences in the individual, which in such cases the social institutions do not fulfil.

Naturally, there are mismatches of this kind in many societies, particularly the industrialized and industrializing ones. But without doubt they occur far more strongly in non-autocratic societies, with their greater individualization, their wider scope for choice and personal responsibility, their more deeply rooted desire for personal independence, that in autocratic societies. Whether veiled or clearly exposed, the symptoms are less concealed in the former than in the latter. They find expression in art and science, newspapers and periodicals, in philosophical discussions as in daily speech.

And it is here, above all, that they present themselves again and again as expressions of an eternal gulf and antithesis between "individual" and "society", a gulf which has its origin in the structures of man and society themselves. Many scholars, not least Freud himself, seem inclined to see in opposites of this kind an unalterable fact of human existence, one of the tragic fundamentals of life with which one has to come to terms, as with pain, sorrow and the death of those one loves. And at the basis of discussions of such problems as something more or less self-evident we constantly find the assumption that they are unalterable, given antinomies between two separate entities always present among human beings. These entities might be thought of as an "extra-social individual" and an "extra-individual society", or as manifestations of an "extra-social nature" confronted by an "unnatural society".

As so often, problems which arise in the course of a socio-historical development and are tied to a particular human situation, present themselves to the people entangled in them as eternal problems of mankind itself. Discrepancies like the one used as an example here are characteristic of societies in which the individual is placed in a strictly controlled but fairly pervasive competition from which physical force is excluded. It is a competition for opportunities which are regarded as valuable and worth striving for by the standard of a fairly unambiguous social scale of values. These opportunities, for one reason or another, remain unattainable to the majority of those who pursue them. But for the individuals who attain them they are associated with rewards of diverse kinds, whether a feeling of fulfilment, property and power, respect and enjoyment, or a combination of these.

The problems which arise for the individual in such a peculiar society are of a peculiar kind. From childhood the individual is trained to develop a fairly high degree of self-control and personal independence. He is accustomed to competing with others; he learns early on, when something earns him applause and causes him pride, that it is desirable to distinguish oneself from others by personal qualities, efforts and achievements; and he learns to find satisfaction in successes of this kind. But at the same time, in all such societies strict limits are set to the manner in which one can distinguish oneself, and the fields in which one may do so. Outside these limits the exact opposite is expected. There, one person is not expected to stand out from others; to do so would be to incur disapproval and often much stronger negative responses. The individual's self-control is therefore directed at not stepping out of line, at being like everyone else, conforming. Often it is no less difficult to conform in one respect than to distinguish oneself in others. It is certainly never an easy matter to strike the right balance between being like all the others in some ways and being unique and unlike them in others. One need only think of the often-discussed problem of the great artist, as dealt with by Thomas Mann, for example, or of outstanding personalities among scholars, political leaders, industrialists and in many other groups, to find examples. In one form or another the attempt to strike this balance brings characteristic tensions with it. But however we consider them, they are not tensions between the non-social, natural needs of the "individual" and the unnatural demands of a "society" outside him, but tensions and difficulties of the individual person, bound up with the peculiar norms of behaviour within his society. These norms form a pattern which in one form or another determines the pattern of his own individual behaviour-control. In a word, these are inherently social discrepancies that find expression in the idea of an eternal tension and gulf between the "inner world" of the individual and the "outer world" of society.

The same applies to the difficulties that arise because the striving to stand out, to achieve something exceptional, to use one's personal gifts and fulfil one's individual life, can only be realized by a minority. Counterposed to the satisfaction that the reaching of such goals gives to a small minority of people, is the muted or clearly felt dissatisfaction of a far larger number who do not achieve what they hoped to in the greater and lesser competitions, who fall short of the aspirations of their youth as they grow older. The feelings of fulfilment in the former are matched by feelings of unfulfilment, boredom, apathy, depression, guilt and the meaninglessness of life in the latter. In this case, too, one of the characteristic forms in which the people concerned interpret their fate is often the idea of a discrepancy between their individual nature and social conditions outside them. The mental structure offered by society of an antithesis between an innate individuality and an "external" society, serves here to explain phenomena which are actually the product of discrepancies within society, the mismatch between the social orientation of individual striving and the social possibilities of fulfilling it.

There is a whole range of phenomena that are put largely out of the reach of observation and thought because such internal social discrepancies are interpreted as antitheses between "nature" and "society", each apparently excluding the other. One might think, for example, of a phenomenon which as yet hardly has a name, the fluctuations in what might be called "social pressure", in particular the "internal pressure" in a society. Whether such fluctuations are connected to the increase in unemployment in industrial states which have unemployment benefit, or with the surplus of university-educated young people in a still largely agrarian country which has not enough posts matching their aspirations, what is involved in this and many other cases is not simply a mismatch between natural, individual needs, such as naturally caused hunger, and the social chances of satisfying them. Indeed, even the starvation of many individual people seems to contribute little to the internal pressure within a society, unless it is associated with strivings that have a social origin and aim. What is involved is a mismatch between such strivings and the chances provided by society of fulfilling them.

VI

To see such discrepancies in this way may help to sharpen our awareness of the inadequacy of many discussions on the question whether the "individual" should be placed higher than "society" or vice versa, as if there really were an either–or choice in the matter. Strictly speaking, one can oppose "individual" and "society" to each other like figures in a puppet show only on a purely linguistic level. And conflicts between groups of states with different value-systems which emphasize one at the expense of the other, contribute not a little to the way such problems are often paraded under an "either–or" banner in everyday life, in the struggle between political parties and even in philosophy, sociology, history and many other disciplines. Because individuals are bound almost as a matter of course to the value-system of one camp or the other, we constantly find that in trying to find out what the relation between individual and society actually *is*, one adopts the battle-cries of the opposed camps, which are mainly concerned with what the relationship *ought* to be.

The factual questions one finds oneself facing on emerging from the smoke generated by the battles over power and values, cannot be formulated in terms of mental constructs intent on expressing everything in terms of diametrical opposites and rigid alternatives. What we see before us are questions of the balance between the demands of the social organization formed by individuals, and the demands of the same individuals *qua* individuals. They are questions such as whether and how it is possible to arrive at a better harmonization between, for example, a state organization with its various organs and aims, and the needs of the individual people comprising it; or a better harmonization of individual goals and needs with the demands of the network of functions they form together.

In the praxis of social life one is constantly concerned with such questions of harmonization and balance. But the conceptual apparatus used in trying to resolve these questions is usually shaped by the adversarial cries of individualism or collectivism, with their diametrically opposed alternatives. If one reflects calmly, it is not difficult to see that in the end both are only possible together. People can only live together harmoniously as a society if their socially formed needs and goals as individuals can find a high level of fulfilment; and a high level of individual fulfilment can only be attained if the social structure they form and maintain by their own actions is so constructed that it does not lead constantly to destructive tensions within groups and individuals. But in practice, societies, particularly in complex industrial states, have not advanced very far in this direction. The adjustment of the social organization to the needs and goals of the individuals within it, and the adjustment of individuals to the demands of the social network as a whole is largely left to chance, or to standard procedures that are taken for granted. On both planes wasteful conflicts, renunciations, failures and collapses are common. There is little ability to harmonize the social shaping of individual needs and aims, for example by education, with the social division of functions. In existing state societies, it seems, one or the other is constantly at a disadvantage. The sharp dividing line one usually draws in personal experience between oneself as an individual and society "out there", the tendency to think of what is referred to by two words as two separate things each of which has a value and meaning of its own, the hardening of social goals into diametrically opposed values, all these contribute to the fact that in action as in thought one takes a priori decisions as to what the relation between individual and society *ought* to be, without making sure that the alternatives between which one is deciding actually match the relationship as it *is*. We have strong convictions about the best cure before we have a diagnosis based on the facts. The question is whether conceptual models that better match the actual relation of individual to society can be extracted from the models overlying them, which primarily express what people believe and wish the relation to be.

By pointing out that the discrepancies we often meet between individual and social demands are not incompatibilities between non-social individual needs and unnatural social demands, but antinomies between personal and social structures immanent to European industrial societies and other societies at the same stage of development, we have taken a step in this direction. The patient work in such human sciences as sociology, psychology and, especially, social psychology, has done much to help us see problems of this kind more clearly. But scientific understanding of the connections between personality structures and social structures is still very limited. Often enough those investigating them seem to start from the assumption that a kind of pre-established harmony automatically exists between the two kinds of structure. It may be that in simpler societies, on which there are numerous studies, the basic pattern of the personality structure or, as Kardiner and Linton called it, the basic structure of the personality, within which individual variants unfold, is less prone to contradictions and in better harmony with the basic structure of the relevant society than in complex industrialized nation states, which are undergoing rapid development. But even in the latter, despite all the differentiation, the common social shaping of individual behaviour, of modes of speech and thought, of affect-control and, above all, of the formation of conscience and ideals through the mediation of an unquestioned national tradition, particularly in the parental home and at school, all this is powerful enough to make the common basic personality structure clearly visible in each member of the society, no matter how they may differ among themselves. Such common features may be easier to recognize in a meeting with members of a different society than with members of one's own. Germans may perceive the common basic pattern of the personality structure more clearly in English, French or American people than in Germans, and conversely, a fact which is not a little characteristic of the whole problem of recognizing social phenomena.

But there are also peculiarities of personality structure that are connected precisely to features of highly differentiated societies. They are enough to indicate that the basic patterns of personality structures are neither necessarily harmonious and contradiction-free in themselves, nor necessarily in complete harmony with such social structures. The high level of individualization, or personal independence and, often enough, of loneliness characteristic of this kind of society, which may even be needed for the maintenance of these societies, frequently does not harmonize very well with the complex and, to the individual, unfathomable network of dependence in which he is enclosed with a growing number of others, largely through his own socially inculcated needs. And the peculiar cross-woven tissue of independence and dependence, of the necessity and ability to decide for oneself on one hand and the impossibility of deciding for oneself on the other, of responsibility for oneself and obedience to the state, can produce considerable tensions. Hand in hand with the desire to be something in one's own right, to which the society of others stands opposed as something external and obstructive, there often goes the wish to stand wholly within one's society. The need to stand alone goes hand in hand with the need to belong. The feeling of participating, being involved, is frequently mingled with one of being uninvolved, detached – "What is all that to me?" And as has already been said, the aim to be something unique and incomparable is often accompanied by the aim not to stand out, to conform. One may admire the increasing control of nature or at least, wittingly or unwittingly, benefit from it, while at the same time complaining about the high degree of self-control and the restraint of short-term impulses which it demands. No one really knows whether and how far the often very peculiar pattern of instinct and affect-control prevailing in many national societies, and the heavy renunciations it frequently imposes on individuals, is actually necessary for the network to function properly, or whether a different, less wasteful and conflict-ridden pattern would be just as effective. Nor does anyone know whether the methods traditionally used in such states to attune the child to life in his society are appropriate to the purpose or not.

But all these questions – the whole cluster of problems that arise in this context – only prove once more how urgent it has become, in the light of the growing factual knowledge in the various human sciences and the problems discussed within them, to investigate the fundamental problem of the relation of society and individual, and to scrutinize the accepted notions associated with these words. Indeed, if the scattered conclusions from research in the various fields are viewed together, it emerges all the more clearly that the categories, the conceptual models normally used in reflecting on such questions, are no longer equal to their task.

Notes

1   We only become fully aware of the peculiarity of a situation in which the standard of "rationality" – to use the common term – is relatively high in thinking about natural events and relatively low in thinking about human-social phenomena, when we rid ourselves of the comfortable idea that this difference is founded in the nature of the matter, in the peculiarity of the two fields of study. We are often content to argue that it is relatively easy to investigate natural phenomena coolly and calmly, with a high degree of self-discipline, because, self-evidently, human feelings are not implicated. We too easily forget that it is only relatively late in their long history that human

beings have been in a position to think "rationally" about natural events, without their feelings, their terror and desires, being directly involved in their concepts. These questions are discussed at more length in Norbert Elias, *Involvement and Detachment*, Oxford, 1987, esp. pp. 6–9, 50–73.

2   See note 3 to Part I above.

Part III
Changes in the We–I Balance
(1987)

I

We make use of different concepts when talking about individuals and when talking about people in groups. In the first case we say a phenomenon is individual, in the second, social. At present the two concepts "individual" and "social" have connotations that suggest they are being used to point not merely to differences but to an antithesis.

Like many other words with Latin roots, the terms "individual" and "social" have representatives in all the European languages. These indicate their common descent from medieval societies with a broad stratum of more or less learned clerics who spoke and wrote a special kind of Latin, at a different stage of development from the classical language. Today the terms "individual" and "social" roll easily enough from the tongues of those who use these European languages. There is not usually any reason to reflect that these terms have not always been a part of the vocabulary of our society – still less of all societies – or to wonder what development, what structural features of our society have led to their emergence and their use as unquestioned means of human communication. Clearly these terms have a particular function in the societies where their use is taken for granted. Like other concepts, they have an instrumental character in these societies, and can therefore serve to bear witness to certain structural peculiarities of these societies. But it takes a considerable effort of detachment from one's own assumptions to realize that there are societies, and have been stages in the development of our society, in which concepts like "individual" and "social" in

155

their present sense do not or did not exist, and to ask oneself what twist of fate, what social development contributed to bringing them into use. Tracing them back, one finds that such concepts often emerge in a very curious manner from the linguistic means at a society's disposal.

As the title of this book implies, it is an error to accept without question the antithetical nature of the two concepts "individual" and "society". The linguistic usage which inclines us to do so is of relatively recent date. It can do no harm to call this usage into question and to demonstrate by a few spot checks that such concepts do not exist simply as of right. One can very briefly sketch their genesis and the conditions of their use.

Let us take as an example the family of concepts with the concept "individual" at its centre. Today, the primary function of the term "individual" is to express the idea that every human being in the world is or should be an autonomous entity, and at the same time that each human being is in certain respects different to all others, and perhaps ought to be different. In the use of this term fact and postulate have no clear dividing line. It is characteristic of the structure of the more developed societies of our day that the differences between people, their I -identity, are valued more highly than what they have in common, their we-identity. The former outweighs the latter. More will be said about this later, but this kind of we–I balance, its clear tilting towards I-identity, is anything but self-evident. At earlier stages of development the we-identity often enough has precedence over the I-identity. The unquestioning way in which the term "individual" is used in conversation in the more developed societies of our day to express the primacy of I-identity may mislead us into assuming that the emphasis is the same in societies at all stages of development, and that equivalent concepts have existed at all times in all languages. That is not the case.

Think, for example, of the classical languages of the Greeks and Romans. In the development of the societies who set their stamp on these languages, the Athenian and Roman states, there were no movements, among the social strata which shaped the language, opposed to the state as such, whereas such movements existed in the more recent development of Europe. Social movements of this kind played a considerable part in the development of the meanings of the terms "individual" and "society" as now used. Inbuilt in the present meanings of both terms is not only the notion of a quite definite and obvious antithesis between individual and society, but also a common, if less obvious, antithesis to the state. The republican Roman state of antiquity is a classical example of a stage of development at which the sense of belonging to family, tribe and state, i.e. the we-identity of the individual person, carried far more weight in the we–I balance than today. Thus, we-identity was hardly separable from the image the language-shaping classes had of the individual person. The notion of a groupless individual, of a person as he or she would be if divested of all we-reference, as he or she would appear if the isolated person were rated so highly that all we-relations, such as family, tribe or state, were deemed relatively unimportant, such a notion was still largely below the horizon in the social praxis of the ancient world.

Consequently, there was no equivalent to the concept "individual" in ancient languages. At the stage of the Athenian and Roman republics, the fact of belonging to a family, or a tribe or state, played an inalienable role in the image of man. In the Roman republic, especially, an often intense rivalry between family representatives for access to state posts can be observed. Everyone is now an individual, irrespective of his position in the state. The negative undertones of the Greek term *idiotes* give us an idea of what the Greeks of the classical age thought of someone who played no part in the public affairs of the state. In the spectrum of meanings encompassed by this term, we find rough equivalents of our terms "private person" or "layman", as well as meanings like "crank", "ignoramus" or "fool". The Latin word *persona* might seem like an equivalent of the modern "individual", but the Latin concept has nothing like the same high level of generality or synthesis as the current terms "person" or "individual'. The Latin term *persona* referred to something quite specific, tangible. It related first of all to the masks of actors, through which they spoke their words. Some scholars incline to the view that the word *persona* is derived from the verb *personare*, to "sound through". That is possible, but no more than a conjecture. From the tangible starting point of the mask there then developed nuances of meaning of *persona*, such as those referring to the role of an actor or to the character of the person he portrayed. But in antiquity the concept *persona* remained fixed at this relatively high level of particularity; it remained, as compared to the modern concept of the person, at a relatively low level of generality. The word *individuum* itself, applied to a person, is unknown in classical Latin. Naturally, the ancient Romans knew as well as we may suppose all other people know that everyone has his peculiarities. They knew that Brutus was different from Caesar, Octavian from Anthony, and no doubt how they were different. But there was clearly no need among the language-forming strata of their society, above all the users of written language, for a comprehensive, universal concept which signified that each person, irrespective of the group to which he or she belonged, was an independent, unique person different from all others, and at the same time expressed the high value placed on such uniqueness. The group identity of the single person, his we-, you- or they-identity, played a much too important role, compared to I-identity, in the social praxis of the ancient world to give rise to a need for any universal concept for the single person as a quasi-groupless entity.

We see here some of the new theoretical tools of sociology directly at work. The instrumental character of concepts and their development is perhaps becoming somewhat clearer. From the standpoint of process-sociology the development of concepts, seen as an aspect of social development, also has an explanatory function. Since we are concerned in this book with the concepts "individual" and "society", it may be of assistance to realize how little we should take it for granted that in the more developed societies of today – and increasingly in the less developed ones –

one is able to manipulate concepts, often quite effortlessly, at a very high level of synthesis.

Earlier, one would probably have referred in this context to concepts "at a very high level of abstraction". But the term "abstraction" is misleading. The concept of abstraction originates from a phase in the development of knowledge when it was tacitly assumed that the single human being, as an isolated individual, could be regarded as the producer, and thus as the absolute originator and starting point of a concept. In that phase it may have seemed conceivable that a single person could convert a single case into a general concept by divesting it of its particularities, by abstraction. In terms of process-theory the situation looks different. The concept of the person did not evolve from the Roman actor-concept of *persona* through individual abstraction performed by a single person. A long social process had been at work, and what emerged from it was not something negative, the stripping of particularities from single cases and the isolation of what was common or general to all. What this process brought about was a synthetic view of many common elements that made a new, previously unknown entity accessible to communication, raised it into the light of understanding. The concept of the person – compared to its ancestor, the Latin *persona* – does not involve a disregarding of certain features; it is a synthesizing view from a new and higher standpoint.

The single human being works on concepts taken from a pre-existing linguistic and conceptual vocabulary that he or she has learned from other people. If this were not so, a person could not rely on being understood by other people when developing an existing language, and thus existing concepts. Individual work to develop concepts further would then be useless. But if one learns to perceive the world, society, language as processes without a beginning, if the subject of concept-forming is no longer seen as a quasi-groupless individual who plucks new concepts from the air, but as the developmental process of a society, often organized as a survival unit such as a tribe or state, one gains a different perspective. One then sees more easily that the transition from more specific or, as was said earlier, more "concrete" concepts (but can concepts ever be "concrete"?) to more comprehensive or general concepts occurs, above all, through a rising to a wider overall view, a higher level of synthesis. This leaves open the question as to the social conditions which make such a rise necessary and possible. It is enough here to point out that all concepts of high generality, existing at a high level of synthesis, are descended from concepts with a far more specific meaning, representatives of a far higher level of particularity and a far lower level of synthesis. Earlier one would probably have said that all "more abstract" concepts stem from "more concrete" ones. But "concrete concepts" are a monstrosity. All concepts, whether representing a lower or a higher level of synthesis, have the character of spoken or written linguistic symbols. To fulfil their function as means of communication and orientation, they must be comprehensible not only by a single person but by a language community, a specific group of people.[1]

Many of our present linguistic means, including the family of concepts grouped around the noun "individual", are of relatively recent date. In medieval Latin words like *individualis* or *individuus* still had meanings located mainly at the lowest level of synthesis. They were used to refer to something indivisible. As late as the seventeenth century one could still speak, for example, of the "Holy individual Trinity". The use of the word *individuus* as a symbol for an indivisible unity was probably linked, in the communication of medieval church scholars, to a further development which probably formed the bridge to the development of the more recent concept of "individual". The word *individuum* was used in connection with problems of formal logic to express a single case in a species – not only human, but any species. But no conclusions could be drawn, it seemed, from isolated statements. *Individua* were therefore regarded as indefinite or vague. In the realm of logic *individua* thus had no very high rank. But for the development of the concept the scholastic term was significant. It is worth saying that in this as in many other cases, for reasons I cannot go into here, scholastic philosophy has made a substantial contribution to the development of a concept at a higher level of synthesis. The medieval term *individuum*, as I have said, did not refer exclusively to human beings. This was probably a seventeenth century development; it made more specific a concept that had previously, in the field of logic and grammar, been used as a universal concept. The church philosophers had seen that everything in this world is in certain respects an individual, i.e. unique. The swallow building its nest under the eaves of my house is unique, an individual. No other swallow is doing this here and now. Each of the wind-blown mountain pines has a unique shape. The fly buzzing across the window here and now is an individual; there is not a single other one doing it. Mont Blanc is unique; there is no other mountain with its shape. Each single entity has its own individual history and its peculiarities. The scholastic philosophers recognized the uniqueness of the single case in a species, and coined a word for it. It proved pregnant with an unforeseeable development.

The problem posed by the concept of the individual may become somewhat clearer if we picture the rise to the level of development attained by scholasticism. How did it happen that the recognition of the uniqueness of all special cases represented by the scholastic concept of the individual was narrowed down again until the concept referred only to the uniqueness of human beings? This clearly happened during the rise of social development to a level where people, perhaps first in specific groups, felt a stronger need to communicate with each other about their uniqueness – and more generally about the uniqueness of each person – about the special quality of their existence as compared to that of all others. The epoch we call the Renaissance was a time when, in the most developed countries in Europe, people were more able than before to rise from their traditional communities to relatively high social positions. Humanists in municipal and state posts, no less than merchants or artists, are examples of the increased social opportunities for individual advancement. At any rate, we then meet in the seventeenth century with the distinction, possibly first among English Puritans, between what is done individually and what is done collectively. This was a preliminary to the further development of the concept which finally led in the nineteenth century, in conjunction with a growing social need for linguistic equivalents for antithetical sociopolitical movements and ideals, to word formations such as "individualism" on one hand and "socialism" and "collectivism" on the other. They contributed much to the situation in recent times where the terms "individual" and "society", with the corresponding adjectives, are used as if they were opposites.

II

If one has been concerned for half a century, as I have, with the problem of the relation of individual and society, it becomes especially clear that this relation is not standing still. During what is, for a researcher's lifetime, a long period, it has changed in certain ways, and is changing further.

Before the Second World War the concept of society usually referred implicitly to a society organized as a state, or perhaps as a tribe. As a legacy of their tradition sociologists carried with them the idea that society and the state were two quite different objects of scholarly investigation. To take account of the fact that the image of experience associated with the concept "society" implied some boundaries to the society, some sociologists spoke of a society as a whole, or as a system. In this way they sidestepped the unwelcome necessity of admitting that the boundaries of a society in relation to others usually coincide with state frontiers or tribal limits. But no matter how much the identity of social boundaries with state or tribal ones was glossed over in sociological terminology, in scientific practice it was usually state societies that acted quite unambiguously as models for what was perceived as society. Not merely the theoretical but the empirical work of sociologists related as a rule to social processes within a state. Even when the development of a society was discussed, it usually referred, as in the case of Karl Marx, to development within a state framework. At most, processes within different states were compared, as in Durkheim's well-known book on suicide. The concept of humanity, on the other hand, was too vague to serve as a sociological framework. It was also tainted with a slight odour of Enlightenment ideals.

This older regime, this earlier stage of sociology, when social units organized as tribes and states were the models for the concept of society, by and large corresponded to social reality. The distances between many states and groups of states before the social development which generated the automobile and air transport and for a good time afterwards, were very great. Telecommunications, radio and television were still in their infancy. Global tourism and goods traffic were relatively limited, and the same was true of the whole network of interdependence between the states of the world. The network has become visibly more dense in the course of the twentieth century. People themselves, however, only perceived this in a very limited, inexact way. They were not used to thinking in terms of social processes. Hardly anyone spoke clearly about the rapidly increasing integration of humanity. It was seldom seen as a long-term, unplanned social process. Thus the shortening of distances, the increasing integration, happened, as it were, in secret. It did not obtrude itself on human experience as a global process of integration.

We can leave open the question how far the transformation in perception has been able to follow the social transformation in the meantime. But as a sociologist one can no longer close one's eyes to the fact that in our time, in place of the individual states, humanity split up into states is increasingly becoming the framework of reference, as a social unit, of many developmental processes and structural changes. Without global frames of reference such processes and structural changes cannot be either adequately diagnosed or adequately explained. The incipient breakthrough to a new level of integration that can be observed on all sides demands a breakthrough to a new level of synthesis in sociology. Everywhere in the world, tribes are losing their function as autonomous survival units. In the course of increasing integration many states are forfeiting a considerable part of their sovereignty. Like other social processes, this global integration can certainly be reversed, and this could happen quite suddenly. But if that does not happen we are entering an era in which it will no longer be individual states but unions of states which will serve mankind as the dominant social unit, as models of what is meant by society, and thus as frames of reference for many sociological studies.

In keeping with this, the problem of the relation of individual and society poses itself in some respects differently now than it did fifty years ago. There were then less than half as many people in the world: more exactly, about 40 per cent of the present world population. The number of people now alive is not without significance for the theoretical and practical discussion of the actual relation of individual and society. 5000,000,000 individuals in this world. Human society, humanity, is, of course, nothing other than the totality of these individuals. But these five billion individuals are not running about singly or in loose groups, as they are depicted in some older sociological theories, including Max Weber's theory of action. Practically all these people are organized in more or less fixed associations. Looking more closely, one soon finds that the large association of humanity consists of a relatively small number of medium-sized associations that we call states. It is not easy to keep pace with the process of state formation in our time. But as a rough guide it can be said that humanity consists of about 150 states. Most of them are organizations embracing several million human individuals; a few have more than 100 million members and there is a single state which contains more than 1,000 million people in a strongly centralized form. All these states are to a greater or lesser degree dependent on each other, whether economically, through the unilateral or mutual threat of violence or through the direct use of violence; or through the spread of models of self-control and other aspects of behaviour and feeling from certain centres, through the transfer of linguistic or other cultural models, and in many other ways.

For sociologists, it seems to me, it is not enough to treat the global frame of reference of many isolated social processes as a model of state. We are not concerned with something static. Human beings are at present involved in an immense process of integration which not only goes hand in hand with many subordinate disintegrations but can at any time give way to a dominant disintegration process. But for the time being the direction is towards a more comprehensive and durable total integration of mankind. It is of great importance for both theoretical and empirical sociological research, and for its application to social practice, to understand the dominant direction of such a process at any time. And certainly not just for sociologists. Mankind's process of learning about the unplanned things happening to it is a slow process which trails considerably behind the social process in which it is engaged at any time. In these circumstances it is especially important not to allow oneself to be misled by wishes and ideals into confusing what one desires as an ideal with what is actually happening. An example may make this clear.

One of the features of many social integration processes from a lower to a higher level is the fact that power is transferred from one level to another. When, in earlier times, self-ruling tribes combined into self-ruling states, the power of the tribal authorities was reduced in favour of that of the state authorities. The individual members of the tribe now lived at a greater distance from the social centres of power which decided over their fate in many respects. The individual members had, in many cases, a chance to participate in the decisions of the tribe. This chance diminishes when the tribes increasingly give up their power and decision-making to the state authorities. Expressed differently, in the course of such integration processes the individual first of all loses power-opportunities in relation to society. Something very similar is now happening in connection with the shift of power from the state level to the continental and global levels. We are at present in an early phase of this advance of integration. But at this stage it is already clear that the individual citizens who in parliamentary democracies have painfully won the right to control their own fates to a limited extent through elections within the state framework, have virtually no chance of influencing events on the global plane of integration – for example, relations between the two superpowers, the United States and the Soviet Union.

Some of my readers may perhaps wish me to tell them only about aspects of mankind's development that are pleasant and hopeful. But such a selection is the true meaning of the *trahison des clercs*. We may or may not welcome the increasing integration of mankind. What is quite certain is that to begin with it increases the impotence of the individual in relation to what is happening at the top level of humanity.

The traditional philosophical debate on individual free will versus determinism has been confined to a discussion, laced with ideals, on the freedom of the human being in relation to human nature. Even this was usually done in a purely speculative way, without the slightest attempt to take account of the state of biological knowledge about the peculiarities of human nature. How limited this approach was is made emphatically clear by the fact that the problem of the restriction of a person's decision-making powers by virtue of living with others, i.e. the sociological aspects of the problem, played a minimal role compared to the natural aspects in the traditional debate conducted by theologians and philosophers. Hence the discussion of freedom always presented itself as being about something immutable, given for all time. With the sociological problem of individual scope for decision the situation is different. This scope can be changed. The individual loss of power when the integration centre and the concomitant powers shift from the tribal to the state level can, within limits, be corrected. It can become the subject of a learning process. But such a learning process takes time. One does not find oneself suddenly at the desired goal. What matters is the direction in which one is going.

We complain about the imperfections of the present central

institutions of mankind, such as the United Nations, treating them as if they represented a final state. We are not astonished that such global institutions have emerged at all. We do not see in them symptoms of a process moving in a particular direction and encompassing the whole of mankind, and so we fail to realize that these experiments with institutions embracing practically all states are stages in a learning process. Unplanned factors reduce distances, increase dependence between states. People cannot simply know, they have to learn what institutions they should create to deal with the problem of global integration, and in most cases they do not learn simply by objective thought processes. Usually they learn by bitter experience. Two world wars were needed to bring the feeble central institutions of the evolving association of states into existence. The hopes of many people, and perhaps the efforts of some of them, are directed at trying to ensure that the bitter experience of a third world war is not needed to push forward the development and effectiveness of these central institutions.

As yet people usually lack a clear perception of the obvious fact that the present shift towards the integration of mankind, which finds expression in such early forms of global institution as the United Nations or the World Bank, is the last movement so far in a very long, unplanned social process, a process leading in many stages from smaller, less differentiated social units to larger, more complex ones. More will be said about this long-term, comprehensive process of social integration. But it may be useful to draw attention right away to a little-noticed aspect of this process, which is of some importance in the present context. With each transition from a less populous, less complex form of the dominant survival organization to a more populous and complex one, the position of individual people in relation to the social unit they form together – in brief, the relation of individual and society – is changed in a characteristic way. If one attempted to present the direction of this change in a somewhat simplified form to make it amenable to more detailed investigation, one might say that the breakthrough to a new dominant form of a more complex and comprehensive type of human organization[2] goes hand in hand with a further shift and a different pattern of individualization. The canon of behaviour, and especially the scope of the identification between person and person, changes with the transition to a new stage of integration in a specific way. The scope of identification increases.

Undoubtedly, the transition to the integration of mankind on a global plane is still at an early stage. But early forms of a new, worldwide ethos, and especially the widening of identification between person and person, are already clearly discernible. There are many signs of the emergence of a new global sense of responsibility for the fate of individuals in distress, regardless of their state or tribe, in short, their group identity. Campaigns for what is at present understood by human rights no doubt draw part of their impetus from political interests in the struggle between the great powers.

But even if politicians place the ethos of human rights narrowly in the service of *raison d'état* today, this may rebound on them tomorrow. Tomorrow the ethos of human rights may turn against those who exploit it for narrow national interests today. Indeed, this would not be the first time the rise to a more comprehensive ethos took its first impetus from being used as a weapon between sub-groups. And there are other signs of early forms of a growing feeling of worldwide responsibility for the fate of human beings. They match the worldwide threat through the development of weapons and, unintentionally, of civil production. A number of private organizations, such as Amnesty International, bear witness to the spread of a sense of responsibility among individuals for the fate of others far beyond the frontiers of their own country or continent.

It is only another aspect of the social change in the same direction that the local mobility of people beyond the borders of their own states, whether as tourists or emigrants, has increased extraordinarily in the course of the twentieth century. This mobility is a mass phenomenon, a possibility open to large sections of the populations of more developed countries (even though in some states individual mobility is still very restricted). Compared to the preceding stages in the development of human survival units, for example, the large, autocratically ruled princely states, the large, more developed nation states with parliamentary government offer their members even now, before the process of integration into a tightly knit worldwide network of states has fully begun, a greater chance of individualization.

III

We may get a clearer picture of this connection between the development of more and more populous and complex types of social unit on one hand and the increasing chances of individualization on the other if we compare the current, latest stage in mankind's development – the division of mankind into about 150 states and their increasing integration into an all-embracing network of interdependence – with an earlier stage, when mankind consisted of a larger number of smaller units. This juxtaposing of a comparatively late configuration of mankind with a much earlier stage demands a certain effort of the imagination, particularly as the evidence is sparse. Nevertheless, such a comparison is indispensable if we are to resist the matter-of-course way in which the problem of the relation of individual and society is so often discussed as a seemingly universal problem on the basis of the experience of the people now alive.

To find the key to this problem it is essential to reconstruct the communal life of earlier people who were biologically exactly like us but were largely without protection. Lacking houses, without permanent settlements, they lived in a constant struggle for survival with other creatures – creatures who were their prey or whose prey they might themselves be. It is useful to picture the life of a group of people who sought shelter in natural caves and who left behind in some of these caves, e.g. in the French Dordogne, large-scale and very lifelike pictures of animals. I realize that one does not identify oneself with these people as a

rule. Expressions like "cavemen", "Stone-Age man" "primi-
tives" or "naked savages" indicate the distance we involuntarily
place between ourselves and these other people, and the not
inconsiderable contempt with which one is apt to look back from
the height of more comprehensive knowledge and the predomi-
nance it gives us over most of the surviving representatives of
these earlier stages. There is no other reason for this distance and
contempt than the somewhat thoughtless egotism it reveals.

The groups which, temporarily or permanently, found shelter
from wind, rain and wild animals under overhanging rocks or,
when they were available, in caves, were probably groups of kin
embracing perhaps twenty-five to fifty people. There may sometimes have been forms of organization that could hold together
100 people for long periods. At any rate, such figures make clear
a factor which is of considerable importance in understanding the
relation of individual and society. In that world, where power was
more evenly distributed between human groups and the manifold
representatives of non-human nature, where the balance of
power between human and non-human beings had not yet tilted
as it did later in favour of human groups with settlements and
dwellings built by themselves, the group had a protective function
for the individual which was both indispensable and unmistakable. In a world where people were exposed to an omnipresent
threat from physically stronger, and perhaps more agile and fleet-
footed animals, a completely isolated person had no great chance
of survival. As in the case of many anthropoid apes, living in
groups had an indispensable survival function for humans too.
People of our species lived in this situation, in this basic dependence on group living, for a far longer stretch of time than the one
we give the name of history: 40,000 or 50,000 years may be an
underestimate – about ten times longer, then, than historical
time.

The *sapiens* form of hominid can be traced back, it seems, to
the Pleistocene. Some palaeontologists may be prevented from
seeing our species as made up of beings living socially from the
start because their picture of man is often based on finds of parts

of the skeletons of isolated individuals. But practically everything we know about prehistoric man indicated that he always lived in groups, and that these groups had a specific structure: that of big game hunters whose women gathered edible plants and roots. This does not apply only to hominids of the *sapiens* species, but to pre-*sapiens* forms. Group living and the special forms of communication and co-operation that *homo sapiens* and his forefathers developed in their communal life, were the basic condition for the successful survival of beings who, in isolation, were notably inferior in muscle power and speed to a large number of beasts of prey, and often enough to their own prey.

The high survival value of group living for each individual member throughout this long prehistoric period of constant struggle with non-human creatures and probably hominid groups as well, has strongly affected the development and the structure of the individual person. The specific meanings of many unlearned signals that a human face can give other people can only be understood by human beings, and are not understood or misunderstood by other beings. The most striking symptom for the group-relatedness of the organic structure of a human individual is the biological disposition of each child to learn a kind of communication which does not link the whole species but possibly only isolated groups. This biological disposition to learn a language which is only understood as a means of communication within a single human society and cannot usually be understood by people outside it, is a unique invention of biological evolution. It has only rudimentary parallels in the structures of other organisms.

The relevant biological structure in human beings, their predisposition to learn a means of communication limited to a single sub-society within the species, and the advancement of this limited means among human beings, indicate very clearly the vital importance that precise understanding between members of a particular group must have taken on during mankind's long formative period.

IV

These examples must be enough to indicate the basic way in which the structure of a single person is related to other people and so to group life. I shall say something more about this later. For the present, the examples may make it easier to understand that discussion of the relation of individual and society must remain one-sided and sterile if carried on solely with regard to the present situation – and thus under the sway of topical issues and ideals. What is needed instead is a process-sociological approach to the problem. Not the least requirement of this approach is that the social sciences should emancipate themselves from the manner of posing problems proper to the natural sciences.[3]

Within the framework of physics, as within the philosophical tradition based on the sciences as its exemplary disciplines, one can largely ignore the self-relatedness and limitations of the present. In physics it is quite adequate to present results based on observations here and now which can claim universal validity. One can legitimately expect experiments done in one's own present time to have the same results as they would have had 2,000, 20,000 or 200,000 years in the past or the future and, who knows, at any point in the universe. That, at any rate, is the assumption on which present, local observations are used to elaborate universal laws or to test such laws.

But this assumption and this procedure are not restricted to the search for regularities, and to the whole style of conceptualization in the realm of the scientific study of natural events. They frequently serve as models for the procedure and concepts of researchers such as philosophers or sociologists, whose task is to investigate human beings and their particular aspects and manifestations. But in this field the basic assumptions underlying the physical mode of research and concept-formation no longer hold good. Applied to research into human beings they are no longer congruent with reality. The relation of individual and society that can be observed in the twentieth century in industrial nation states that embrace more than a million and perhaps more than 100 million people, the personality structures and the whole group-formation at this stage, cannot be used as an experimental model with the aid of which universal statements about human personality structures, social forms or the relation of individual and society can be even tentatively made or tested. In the many thousands of years during which people lived in small groups probably mostly of less than 100 people, the relation between the individual and his group was in certain respects quite different from what can be observed in the far more populous survival units of the present. In the earlier groups no one knew, or could know, that people are able to use natural materials to construct protective dwellings. We could only ascertain what, if anything, was universal in the relation of individual and society if we had as our frame of reference a model leading from the earliest stages of the present human species over a stretch of about 10,000 years to the current stage of development.

Even in the physical sciences there is a growing need to use a model of the evolution of the universe as a frame of reference for observations and experiments made at a certain time and place. But on the plane of inanimate nature the need for a model of cosmic evolution is not so urgent because the tempo of physical evolution, compared to the development of human societies, is extraordinarily slow. One can quite successfully use general laws as means of orientation and forget that they may not apply in the same way to all stages of the evolution of the universe. But the situation is different when investigating human phenomena. The speed at which human groups, i.e. the relations of people to each other, change is comparatively high. One cannot ignore changes in human groups and the corresponding changes in the personality structures of individual people when making universal statements about human beings. In this case it is necessary to include a picture of the development of social and personality structures as a framework for one's study.

The process-sociological approach is based on the realization that on the plane of human groups, of relations between people, one cannot proceed with the aid of concepts, or a process of conceptualization, of the same kind as those used on the level of atoms or molecules and their relations to each other. In the latter field concepts are formed on the basis of classical laws on the assumption that the same regularities that can be observed in the present are to be observed in all places and times, past, present and future, in exactly the same way. The classical form of laws and law-like concepts reflect the uniformity of the inanimate matter forming the physical universe. The same is true of that integration level of the universe represented by the biological structures of human beings. However, the frame of reference here is no longer the developing physical universe. These structures only appear within it, as far as we know, at a limited time and in a limited place. But whenever and wherever they occur, they are essentially identical in structure and dynamics. Blood circulation and brain structure, birth and death are shared by all people. But this can no longer be said of the structure and dynamics of the groups formed by human beings, nor, therefore, of language. These can change relatively quickly. They are different at different times and in different places. To orientate oneself on this integration-plane of the universe it is of little help to look around for laws, or concepts functioning as laws, applicable to the human world in the same way in all times and places. The task which this integration level sets human beings seeking orientation is to discover the order of change in the course of time, the order of successive events, and to seek concepts with which people can communicate about individual aspects of this order. The calendar is a good example of a means of orientation that relates to the order of succession in the change of human societies. The structure of human societies in the ninth century BC differed in specific ways from that of the dominant societies 10,000 years later, as that of the European societies of the nineteenth century differed from that of these societies in the twentieth. But in each case the later structure had the first as its precondition; it did not emerge necessarily from the first, but the first was a necessary precondition for the emergence of the last.

And the same applies to the relation of individual and society in the two cases.

I am quite aware, however, that in requiring that the element of succession in the development of human groups be respected, one is inviting special difficulties of communication. The concept of social development currently bears a stigma deriving from the image of this development predominant in the eighteenth and nineteenth centuries. Anyone who picks up this concept again at the end of the twentieth century and in anticipation of the twenty-first, i.e. at a higher twist of the spiral, risks incurring the contempt of the generation that grew up during the great, traumatic collapse of the old concept of development – the concept which promised the constant progress of mankind rising in a straight line to a happier state. Contaminated with the stigma of disillusion, concepts like "progress" and "development" seemed to have become unusable for research.[4] The collective disappointment that the faith in the ideals associated in an earlier epoch with the ideas of "progress" and "social development", and still affecting their meanings, had been so conspicuously unfulfilled, produced a certain blindness to the fact that they do not actually refer to obsolete, disappointing ideals but to simple, demonstrable facts. For example, it is difficult to deny that human knowledge of natural processes has progressed over the centuries, not least in the present one. But no sooner has one said this than one can often observe an automatic defensive reaction. "Maybe," the answer goes, "but are people any happier for this progress?" The factual point is unimportant compared to the disappointment of which the idea of progress reminds us.

Sociologists, too, joined in the chorus of disappointment. Instead of endeavouring to evolve a fact-based theory of social development undistorted by ideals and disappointed hopes, with a few half-hearted exceptions they simply threw the development of human societies out of their social theories. They fell back on static theories based on the tacit assumption that universal theories of human society could only be built up on the basis of observations of our own society here and now. In other words, instead of the process theories appropriate to the subject matter, they placed theories and concepts with the character of laws at the centre of their work. In so doing they deprived themselves of a conceptual tool which is quite indispensable in studying human societies, not just in the past but in the present. For unlike animal societies which are species-specific and which, apart from slight variants, only change when the genetic equipment of their representatives changes, human societies are in permanent flux; they are subject to constant changes in one direction or another.

The relation of individual and society, too, is anything but immobile. It changes as mankind develops – but not in the way one might be prepared for by the kind of change studied by historians. The change we are concerned with here is a structured change in one of two opposed directions. Precisely this is what one attempts to convey by the fact-orientated use of the concept of social development. The question whether people become happier in the course of this change is not under discussion here. We are concerned with understanding the change itself, its direction and perhaps later even its causes.

V

As no fully worked-out model of human development which is both fact-based and verifiable exists at present, I earlier made use of a hypothetical working model of a very early stage of social development. Freud sometimes spoke of a "primal horde". One might perhaps speak of the stage of cave-dwelling big-game hunters. At this stage the individual person is far more closely and inescapably tied to his social group. A person on his own, a person without a group, had no great chance of survival in that wilder world. That does not mean that group life at that time was more peaceful and free of conflicts than now, just because the individual's dependence on his society was so much more obvious. All it means is that only those groups in the chain of generations survived who succeeded in arriving at a *modus vivendi*, a certain balance between conflict and collaboration.

But we do not need to rely on hypothetical models of developmental stages whose representatives, as far as can be seen, are extinct, to find evidence of differences in the relation of the individual person to his or her society at different stages of development. Such differences are to be found in our own time, if the relation of individual and society in the more developed societies and in the less developed ones is compared.

The lack of knowledge about this kind of difference is a serious obstacle to less developed countries in their efforts to rise to the level of the more developed countries. The necessity of this rise – and it is emerging more and more clearly as a necessity – is usually expressed by catchwords such as "modernization". This directs attention to development in the sense of technical or economic progress, the introduction of machines or changes in economic organization which promise an increase in the national product. Less attention, as a rule, is given to the fact that in the course of such a development process the whole position of the individual in his society, and thus the personality structures of individuals and their relations to each other, are changed in a specific way. It may be that here too one is trying to evade the question of social development since it would touch on sore points in our present social life – points which are therefore placed under taboo. Thus people forbid themselves, for example, to talk of "less developed" countries, to avoid offending their inhabitants, preferring the vague, dissembling term "developing countries", as if the more developed countries were not also in the process of developing and so could also be termed developing countries. But one in no way helps the less developed countries to develop further by excluding from public discussion their characteristic structures, and therefore the problems entailed by the transition from one stage to another. Modifications to the personality structure, changes in the position of the individual in his society that occur in the course of such development, create problems that are among the most serious obstacles to such a transformation. They are little discussed – less, at any rate, than the problems known under the headings "economic" or "political". In this connection, where they serve merely as an example of the developmental aspects of the relation of individual and society, I can only allude to them very briefly.

In the comparatively less developed countries the relation of the individual person to family, community and state is usually different in a specific way from the corresponding relationship in more developed countries. In the former the single human being is usually more tightly bound to his family, which in this case usually has the form of an extended family, and his native village or town than in the latter. In many, though certainly not in all the less developed countries, the state represents a relatively new level of integration. The extended family and the native village are the older focal points of the personal we-identity of the individual. If we consider the relation of I-identity and we-identity, we might say that in all countries, both more and less developed, both are present, but in the former the accent on I-identity is stronger and in the latter the accent is on the pre-state we-identity, whether the family, the native village or the tribe. Among the older generation in states which only recently became independent, we-identity in relation to the state is often relatively weak, involving few positive feelings. This changes in the younger generation, but often without at first causing the strong emotional attachment to family, kin, birthplace or tribe to disappear. A special kind of problem arises in the case of Japan, and perhaps in other Asiatic societies in the course of modernization. So far, the shift of the we–I balance in favour of I-identity is less pronounced there than in western countries, with noticeable advantages for their competitiveness.

The change in the we-identity that takes place in the course of the transition from one stage of development to another can also be elucidated in terms of a conflict of loyalties. The traditional conscience-formation, the traditional ethos of attachment to the old survival unit of family or clan – in short, the narrower or broader kin group – dictates that a more well-off member should not deny even distant relations a degree of help if they ask for it. High officials in a newly independent state thus find it difficult to refuse kinsmen their support if they try to obtain one of the coveted state posts, even a lowly one. Considered in terms of the ethos and conscience of more developed states, the preferment of relations in filling state posts is a form of corruption. In terms of the pre-state conscience it is a duty and, as long as everyone does it in the traditional tribal struggle for power and status, a necessity. In the transition to a new level of integration, therefore, there are conflicts of loyalty and conscience which are at the same time conflicts of personal identity.

A process-sociological approach which brings human problems into the field of study requires us, as we see here, to move to a further level of detachment – a detachment both from the object of research and from the researcher, oneself. Personal involvement through their own consciences makes researchers to whom the habits of their own state have become second nature liable to apply the form and development of the latter as a pattern and standard when viewing the state forms of all other countries. The social model of the more developed state, the social praxis prevailing in it and the personality structure and individual conscience connected with it, are taken completely for granted. It is often taken as a dictate of eternal reason that in all more developed states the filling of posts by relatives should give way to appointment on individual merit. But, as we see, what is realistically possible and necessary, and in that sense reasonable, can differ at different levels of a social development process.

We have here an example of how a certain stage in a process of state formation can favour individualization, the greater emphasis on the I-identity of the individual person, and the detachment of that person from the traditional groupings. As long as one denies oneself access to the sequence of stages in a social development, one is unable to explain the corruption in "developing countries". One then has no option but to join in the chorus of those who loudly or quietly deplore the recurrence of these forms of patronage and favour in newer states. The frequent charge that these states are belittled by being called "less developed" is quite misplaced. The opposite is the case. It would be denigrating them not to speak of them in this way, so closing one's mind to the structure of the change these groups are undergoing as societies and as individuals in the transition from one stage of development to another. It is also of importance to social praxis that one should not allow concern with the purely technical or economic problems of this restructuring to cause us to forget the human problems.

A comparative procedure – and every study of developmental processes demands such a procedure – shows up more clearly not only the structures of what may be earlier stages from the point of view of the observer, but also the social structures at the observer's own stage. It is not wholly unimportant for those living within the organized form of a more developed state if the social make-up of those within this structure loses some of its self-evident quality. To see the importance it has for the make-up of each individual person to have grown up as a citizen of one of the more advanced industrial states can contribute much to our taking this make-up less for granted and placing it in the range of subjects one thinks about and questions. Comparisons help.

At earlier stages of social development the individual was, as we have seen, far more tightly bound to the groups into which he was born. Individual people were mostly tied to pre-state units, kin, birthplace or tribe, for life, or at least more tightly than now, because they were the groups from which they could expect help and protection in dire need. In the more developed societies, which means, not least, those which are richer as such, but richer above all in social capital, the integration level of the state has increasingly absorbed this function of last refuge in extreme need. But in relation to the individual citizen the state has a quite peculiar double function, which at first sight seems self-contradictory. On one hand it irons out the differences between people. In the state registers and offices, the individual is largely divested of his or her distinctive personality. The individual is a

name with a number, a taxpayer or, as the case may be, a person
seeking help and protection, which the state authorities can grant
or refuse. But although the state apparatus in this way embeds
the individual in a network of rules which is by and large the same
for all citizens, the modern state organization does not relate to
people as sisters or uncles, as members of a family group or one
of the other pre-state forms of integration, but to people as
individuals. At the present, latest stage of development the
process of state formation makes its own contribution to a new
advance of mass individualization.

But the extent and pattern of this individualization differ
widely according to the structure of the state and particularly the
distribution of power between government and governed, state
apparatus and citizens. In the dictatorial states of the east, as in
dictatorships of any kind, the state rules enfold the individual
citizen so tightly, that the reciprocal control between rulers and
ruled is so weak, the citizen's scope for decision, and thus the possibility of personal individualization, is relatively limited. Especially
in public life external control heavily outweighs the self-control of
the individual, who is often thrown back on the private sphere.
And even in this sphere the chances of individualization are
further narrowed by the state monopoly of information, education, rights of association and assembly, etc. The scope for self-
control, the personal freedom of choice offered by a certain kind
of state to its members, is an important criterion for the degree of
individualization. Among the peculiarities of a dictatorial regime
is the development of a specific social make-up in the individuals
living under the regime. They are highly attuned to external
control and often feel disorientated at first if this weakens or
disappears. As personal initiative, the individual capacity to take
decisions, is less socially rewarded in the framework of such a
state, and perhaps disapproved of or even punished, such a
regime often has a self-perpetuating character. The people living
in this structure are often made more or less insecure, get into
conflict with their consciences, when required in one way or

another to show a greater degree of self-regulation. Their social make-up makes them tend involuntarily to re-establish the familiar external control, as by a strong leader.

A short digression on the problem of the individual habitus or make-up may be indicated here. The concentration of process-sociology on human beings gives scientific access in this and other cases to problems which are known from the pre-scientific stage of knowledge but cannot be properly explored because of the lack of scientific concepts. Concepts like "social personality structure" or "stage and pattern of individual self-regulation" are among those that can be useful here. In particular, the concept of the social make-up or habitus which I introduced earlier has a key role in this context. In combination with the concept of increasing or decreasing individualization, it enhances our chances of escaping the either/or approach that often finds its way into sociological discussions of the relation of individual and society. If it, and the very similar concept of the social personality structure are understood – and properly applied – it is easier to understand why the old habit of using the terms "individual" and "society" as if they represented two separate objects is misleading. One then no longer closes one's eyes to the fact, that is well enough known outside the field of science, that each individual person, different as he or she may be from all others, has a specific make-up that he or she shares with other members of his or her society. This make-up, the social habitus of individuals, forms, as it were, the soil from which grow the personal characteristics through which an individual differs from other members of his society. In this way something grows out of the common language which the individual shares with others and which is certainly a component of the social habitus – a more or less individual style, what might be called an unmistakable individual handwriting that grows out of the social script. The concept of the social habitus enables us to bring social phenomena within the field of scientific investigation previously inaccessible to them. Consider, for example, the problem that is communicated in a pre-scientific way by the concept of national character. This is a habitus problem *par excellence*. The idea that the individual bears in himself or herself the habitus of a group, and that it is this habitus that he or she individualizes to a greater or lesser extent, can be somewhat more precisely defined. In less differentiated societies, such as the Stone Age hunter-gatherer groups, the social habitus may have had a single layer. In more complex societies it has many layers. Someone may, for example, have the peculiarities of a Liverpool-English or a Black Forest-German European. It depends on the number of inter-locking planes in his society how many layers are interwoven in the social habitus of a person. Among them, a particular layer usually has special prominence. It is the layer characteristic of membership of a particular social survival group, for example, a tribe or state. In members of a society at the developmental stage of a modern state this is referred to by the expression "national character". In members of societies on the way to becoming a modern state, tribal characteristics can often be distinguished – in Nigeria, for example, the social habitus of the Ibo or the Yoruba. At present, it is more pronounced than the common features of all Nigerians, whereas in the German Federal Republic or the Netherlands and France, despite strong countervailing move-ments, the regional differences between people are fading in relation to national ones as integration advances.

VI

The I–we identity that was discussed earlier forms an integral part of the social habitus of a person, and as such is open to individualization. This identity represents the answer to the ques-tion "Who am I?", both as a social and as an individual being. State-societies reach a level of development where organization has advanced to a point where each new-born child must be registered with the state if he or she is to be later recognized as a state citizen, and needs a birth certificate on many occasions while growing up and during adult life. In such societies, the most elementary answer to the question of an individual's I-identity, the question "Who am I?", is the name-symbol in which he or she is registered at birth. Of this name a person can, of course, say: "Hubert Humbert, that's me and no one else." Normally, no one else has this name. But this kind of name, with its two components the forename and the surname, indicates a person both as a unique individual and as a member of a particular group, his or her family. And while on one hand the name gives the individual person a symbol of his or her uniqueness and an answer to the question who that person is in his own eyes, it also serves as a visiting card. It indicates who one is in the eyes of others. From this angle, too, we see how indissoluble a person's existence as an individual being is from his or her existence as a social being. One could not distinguish oneself from other people as an individual if there were no other people. I have already pointed out on many occasions[5] that the word "I" would be meaningless if, when saying it, one did not have in mind the personal pronouns referring to other people as well. The double form of the name shows very clearly what is really obvious: that each individual person emerges from a group of other people whose names he bears in combination with the individualizing forename. There is no I-identity without we-identity. Only the weighting of the I–we balance, the pattern of the I–we relation, are variable.

It may be useful to add that the concept of human identity relates to a process. This can be easily overlooked. At first sight I- and we-statements might seem to have a static character. I, one might say, am always the same person. But it is not true. At fifty Hubert Humbert is a different person than at ten. If he says "I" at fifty, it does not refer to the person he was at ten. On the other hand, the fifty-year-old person stands in a very special, unique relation to the ten-year-old. At fifty a person no longer has the same personality structure as at ten, yet is the same person. For the fifty-year-old person has emerged directly from the one-year-old, the two-year-old, and thus the ten-year-old, in the course of a specific development process. This continuity of development is the condition of the identity of the ten-year-old and fifty-year-old person.

The conceptual problem of human identity throughout life is difficult, indeed insoluble, as long as individual reflection has at its disposal no fairly clear, socially evolved concept of process and, especially, of development. When Hume remarks that he cannot understand that the child he once was and the grown-up he now is are one and the same person, we can sympathize with his dilemma. At his time the theoretical tools needed for people to communicate about, and therefore to understand, development processes were in their infancy, at a very early stage of development. An enormous collective effort of thought was needed before a concept at a comparatively low level of synthesis, the concept of de- or en-velopment, could be fashioned into a concept at a higher synthesis-level and made accessible to social communication. The concept of developing first referred to very tangible aspects of social praxis at a low level of synthesis. Specific needs of human understanding led to the further elaboration of the concept of development as a symbol of processes acting in a particular direction, such as the process of growing up or the changing of mankind in a specific direction. They were first understood as a kind of unfolding of a seemingly identical core, comparable to a baby being unwrapped from its nappies. In the course of time it became possible to produce a communicable concept that could be elaborated. In a collective process of thought and observation over generations it was gradually made more reality congruent, and thus more easily usable in social praxis. But at the time when Hume was trying to elaborate his experiences and observations at the high synthesis-level of philosophy, the idea of development was not seen, as it now is, as a familiar part of the social habitus, a part of the intellectual equipment of an educated person. The problem of the relation between different stages in the development of one and the same person, the peculiar intertwinement of identity of person and difference of personality, was at that time quite insoluble.

It is not a personal achievement if one is now able to say somewhat more about the peculiar relation between a person as a child and the same person as an adult. Concepts like that of development, already a part of social usage, and that of I–we identity, which has yet to become accepted in the same way, give us something to hold on to. But they still leave much to be desired. They are anything but a finished product; they are, in other words, ready for further elaboration by future generations.

The problem of individual identity throughout life cannot be intellectually grasped, as may now be more clearly seen, until one takes account of the process-nature of a human being, and until people have at their disposal adequate conceptual tools, linguistic symbols for identifying development processes. At the present stage in the development of process-sociological theory, the way the different aspects of a person's personality development interact and interlock is not clearly understood. The biological, psychological and sociological aspects of this development are the subject of different disciplines working independently. The specialists thus usually present them as existing separately. The real task of research, however, is to understand and explain how these aspects are interwoven in the process, and to represent their interlocking symbolically in a theoretical model with the aid of communicable concepts.

The process of development and its symbolic representation, the process as such and as the object of individual experience, are likewise intertwined and inseparable. As an example of the process per se, one might first point to the fact that each later phase of the development process undergone by an individual person presupposes the continuous sequence of the preceding stages. It is true of human beings as of other processes that one cannot attain the age and form of a thirty-year-old without passing through all the preceding ages and their forms. Continuity of the development process is one of the preconditions of the identity of a person in the course of a process stretching over years. The later form of a person necessarily emerges from the sequence of preceding forms. But it does not necessarily follow it. A person can die before reaching the later stage. The later personality structure is dependent on the development-flow of the earlier ones, but with an initially considerable scope for variation that later gradually diminishes.

In the case of a human being, the continuity of the process-sequence as an element of I-identity is interwoven, to a greater degree than in any other living creature, with another element of I-identity: the continuity of memory. This faculty can preserve learned knowledge and therefore personal experiences in earlier phases as means of active control of feeling and behaviour in later phases to an extent which has no equivalent in non-human organisms. The immense capacity for the selective preservation of experiences at all ages is one of the factors that play a decisive role in the individualization of people. The greater the scope for differences in the experiences engraved in the memories of individuals in the course of social development, the greater the chance of individualization.

But to speak of the continuity of development anchored in memory as a condition of a person's I-identity is not enough. A development does not take place in abstraction. Each memory has a substrate. I-identity is not made possible only by memory of oneself and knowledge of oneself that are engraved in one's own brain; its basis is the whole organism, of which the brain is a part – though certainly a central part. This organism is the substrate of a development process which a person undergoes. It is really this organism to which a person refers in conversation when saying "I" or "we" to denote or include himself, whereas he uses other personal pronouns in the second or third persons to refer to other human organisms. The I-identity of people depends to a very large extent on their being aware of themselves as organisms, in other words, as highly organized biological units. Owing to a peculiarity of their bodily organization, people are in a position to distance themselves from themselves as a physical organization in observing and thinking about themselves. Because of this peculiarity of their physical organization, which allows them to perceive themselves as temporal-spatial figures among other such figures, as bodily existing people among other such people, they are able to characterize their own position by using the symbol "I", among other ways, and the position of others by symbols like "you", "he" or "they".

This peculiarity of human nature, this ability of people, based on their physical organization, to confront themselves, with the aid of their knowledge and language symbols, as if they were people or objects among others, has led to their often having a curiously split image of themselves. Their verbal symbols are formed as if they themselves, as someone contemplating their own person from a certain distance, and as that which they contemplate from a distance, were different beings which might even have separate existences. Thus one speaks of oneself in one's capacity as object of observation by means of terms such as "my body", while in relation to oneself as a being able to observe oneself from a distance one uses terms such as "my person", "my soul" or "my mind". It is not always said with sufficient clarity that these concepts represent two different perspectives of one's own person as if they were two different objects often enough existing separately. The simple use of the term "my body" makes it appear as if I were a person existing outside my body who has now acquired a body in much the same way as a garment.

As a result of this deep-rooted dualistic tradition it can be misleading to say that I am my body. It is misleading because the concept "body", used in this context, is ambiguous. One can speak of a pyramid as a body, or of a star or a molecule. The ambiguity of the formulation that I myself am my body derives from the fact that the term "body" can refer both to pieces of lifeless and relatively unorganized matter and to highly organized biological units and thus to the most complex organisms. The statement "I am my body" or "I am identical to my body" can, therefore be understood to mean: "I am nothing but a piece of unorganized matter". And indeed, the idea that the living human organism, which, as long as it functions as an organism – i.e. until it dies – is constantly in flux, engaged in a development, a process, could be reduced simply to the forms of lifeless matter, undoubtedly plays a considerable role among the philosophical schools of our day. It may therefore be necessary to safeguard our statement that we refer only to two different perspectives and not two different forms of existence when we speak of our own body and our own person, from materialistic reduction.

In this connection one might recall a circumstance which, significantly, often escapes notice. In talking about the human body one often overlooks the fact that a person's head, and especially his or her face, is an integral part of this body. As soon as one realizes this one gains a better understanding of the nature of human I-identity. For the developing individual face of a person plays a central part, perhaps the most central part, in his or her identity as this particular person. Although the particular form of the other parts of the body are, no doubt, also of importance in identifying a person, no part is so unequivocally at the centre of a person's I-identity, both in the consciousness of others and for the person himself, as his face. And it is the face which shows most clearly to what extent I-identity is bound up with the continuity of development from childhood to extreme old age.

Indeed, the development process a person's face undergoes from childhood to old age can serve as a prototypical example of a certain type of this process. It changes, but from a certain age on it takes on peculiarities which make it possible to identify a human face as always the same face, a person as always the same person, despite all the changes of ageing. The old logic possibly gives rise to the expectation that something absolutely immutable forms the hard core of all changes, the unchanging, undeveloping core of all development. The example of the development of a person, particularly the face, may perhaps make it easier to understand the fact that in the course of such a process there need not be anything that stands still and is absolutely unchangeable. The identity of the developing person rests above all on the fact that each later phase emerges in an unbroken sequence from an earlier phase. The genetic control that directs the course of a process is itself a part of this process. And the same applies to memory, both conscious and unconscious. Although memory content is to a certain extent fixed, so becoming an element helping to shape the character and the face, it also changes in specific ways as the person matures and grows old.

VII

Human beings share their property of being a kind of process, of course, with many other organisms. What distinguishes them from other organisms, whether ants or apes, is not least their capacity, already mentioned, to produce a mirror effect. They can in a sense step out of and opposite to themselves, so that they can see themselves as if in the mirror of their consciousness. A person is for himself or herself at once an I, a you and a he, she or it. A person could not be an I for himself or herself, without at the same time being a person who can stand opposite himself or herself as a you or he, she, it. Biologists are often concerned with the peculiarities that human beings may have in common with anthropoid apes or perhaps with rats. The unique feature with which the dynamic of biological evolution has equipped human beings and which distinguishes them from all other organisms, can be neglected by such an approach. And indeed, concepts like "knowledge", "awareness", "self-consciousness" and many others are often used as if what they refer to has no biological foundation. The human body thereby appears unconscious, or devoid of consciousness; it is all a bit confused. If one speaks of one's body, it means nothing other than that one considers oneself as something existing in the third person, as if one were a he, she or it. Certainly, the ability of people to step consciously out of themselves and to confront themselves as something existing in the second or third person is mobilized in societies at different stages of development to a very different extent and in very different ways: but it is the precondition of making tools and still more of passing on knowledge, including knowledge about oneself – an act which is detached from the momentary situation of the subject of knowledge within the unbroken chain of generations.

The approach of ethologists and other specialists in animal psychology, which investigates all human behaviour with the same theoretical tools that have proved adequate and fruitful in studying sub-human organisms, can yield only limited results. It distracts attention from a decisive factor. In the biological species of man, structural qualities that humans share with animals and which, in other words, prove their undoubted descent from non-human organisms, are indissolubly interwoven with structural qualities which represent an evolutionary innovation. These features are uniquely, specifically human and are absent in the biological equipment of all other organisms on this earth, as far as is now known. The fact that human beings can be reduced neither to matter nor to animals, although they consist of matter and have evolved from animals, that, in a word, they represent a breakthrough to new and singular organic structures within the continuous evolutionary process, is left aside by such reductionist endeavours. The problems posed by this as by any other breakthrough of the blind, unplanned evolutionary process to novel biological structures lie fallow in the no-man's-land between the disciplines.

What survival value did it have, one might ask, for humans to learn to communicate with each other in a quite new, unique way? At the human level organisms acquired not only the opportunity but the need to use a group-specific language as their chief means of communication. The learning of a language in itself presupposed a biological structure that made self-detachment possible. Thus the human descendants of animals attained, with their group-specific language, the possibility also of saying, in one linguistic form or another, "I" of themselves and "we" of each other, and to speak of others in the second or third persons singular or plural. In the communication of all other organisms, by contrast, unlearned, i.e. innate, signals play the main part. Many scholars have tried in vain to teach anthropoids elements of a society-specific language, without clearly realizing the difference between the dominance of species-specific and society-specific forms of communication. The stages of biological evolution that led to this radical change are unknown at present. The least one can do is to pose the question how a change so rich in consequences could come about. What act of fate brought about the development of the biological structures that enabled the human descendants of animals to achieve the self-detachment necessary in order to learn to speak and to say "I" of themselves? And further, what act of fate enabled the relatively stiff faces of our animal forebears to change into the extraordinarily mobile, individualizable faces that are among the unique biological features of man?

We do not know these acts of fate. We do not know what peculiar circumstances over millions of years led to humans being, as far as we know, the only species of organism to have acquired biological equipment making it not only possible but necessary to be able to produce and understand, as their main means of communication, sound configurations which differed from group to group. Nor do we yet know which recurring events over millions of years led to humans being biologically endowed with a highly individualizable physiognomy, with a ductile facial musculature that can take on a different imprint according to individual experience. But the events of this evolution are clearly understood. Human beings are the only organism so far known who use a society-specific rather than species-specific primary means of communication, and they are also the only species known to us with a part of the body so capable of bearing a different individual stamp that, by means of it, hundreds of individuals are able over a long period, and often for life, to recognize each other as such, as different individuals.

The exponents of palaeo-anthropology and the other sciences concerned with the biological evolution of human beings do not always give these two peculiarities of the human species now living the attention they deserve. That is not surprising, as their work concentrates on information that can be derived from the few remains of past anthropoids and early forms of man. It is undoubtedly difficult and perhaps impossible to glean from these few remnants information on the evolution underlying the society-specific human forms of communication and the individualization of human faces. But for many other human scientists, particularly sociologists, it is quite indispensable to pay attention to the fact that humans differ from other organisms by these two features rooted in their biological organization – the dominance of a society-specific form of communication, acquired by learning, over the species-specific form; and a moulding of the parts of the body around the mouth and eyes that can be learned, and therefore individualized.

No doubt the biological organization of human beings has a large number of unique features. The upright gait, the development of the front legs into arms and hands which are unusually mobile, the bifocal sight and other aspects of this kind are frequently noted. But the distinguishing features of humans that have been given most attention up to now are usually those which are of exclusive interest to biologists and the exponents of related disciplines. They concern the individual organism. Relatively little notice is taken of the fact – certainly not unknown in itself – that humans, just like their animal forefathers, are social beings. Their biological organization is thus attuned to their living together. The division of academic disciplines, the prevalent orientation of biology, and of medical science, towards the organism in isolation and species-specific structures of organisms, have led to a regrettable confusion in the linguistic and intellectual tradition. It gives the impression that the single human organism or, as one calls it, the body of a human being, as seen in the anatomy class and as examined by the doctor, acts as model for what is understood by the individual. This, the form existing in time and space, is taken as the natural datum; this, the single organism, is considered real. The communal life of people, their society, its structures and processes appear, by contrast, as not given by nature and not actually real. A human being, it is implied, could manage perfectly well if he or she lived permanently alone without society, as a single organism. This is how the majority of biologists visualize him, as do palaeontologists in their skeleton finds. In this way academic specialization contributes to constructing an inadequate conceptual framework, to positing nature and society as opposites.

It is not unimportant, therefore, to point to organic structures which clearly indicate a human being's natural attunement to living with others. Of course, the sexual features already point in this direction. The fact, in particular, that the human sexual urge is no longer tied to limited periods, may play a part in the particularly close kind of socialization of the species. But the uniqueness, the special closeness of human socialization shows itself above all in the unique form of communication of humans. They alone understand each other through languages which differ in different societies, and through a facial moulding which makes it possible to identify a particular person even after an interval of years as this unique individual.

We can leave it to the twenty-first century – and, let us hope, to a collaboration by people from all parts of the world – to find a convincing answer to the question under what circumstances a blind, unplanned natural process produced such a unique form of communication among organisms; and, closely bound up with it, a unique differentness and malleability of the parts around the eyes, nose and mouth, so that, especially from the viewpoint of group membership, each person can be recognized merely by looking at them as a particular person distinct from all others. We do not know how these and some other distinguishing features of a species of organisms which have gained a kind of dominance over their planet and its environment came about. But this fact need not deter anyone from paying attention to these natural features of humans in forming a picture of the human being and so of herself or himself.

Detailed discussion of the function and the consequences of the natural characteristics of people that enabled them to communicate by learned languages takes us too far outside the framework of this book. It must be enough to point out in a few sentences that two other unique features of humans are closely bound up with this dominance of communication through symbols. These features are not genetically fixed, although they are based on a genetically fixed disposition. The two features I have in mind are, first, the ability to transfer a symbolic record of social knowledge from one generation to another, this knowledge being changeable and so capable of growth; second, the lack of a biologically fixed, i.e. species-specific, form of socialization, or, expressed positively, the presence of a form of communal life that can be changed in conjunction with learning processes, and is thus capable of development.

Here I must confine myself to a few observations on facial moulding as one example of the peculiarity of human individualization, and particularly of the I- and we-images. As I have said, the face, more than any other part of the body, is the display board of the person. Within the communal framework – for all people have faces – it makes visible the special nature of the single person. But this is more the case for members of one's own group and their descendants than for those of other groups. If a face has features deviating too far from the norm of one's own group, if, for example, the skin pigmentation or the musculature around the eyes is different from one's own, the perception of the more striking biological features of an alien group often overrides the perception of the less striking, subtler ways in which the faces of members of this group differ. One might perhaps suppose that the primary function of a different individual moulding of the human face was as a means of identifying well-known members of small groups, in conjunction with its function as a means of informing us about their intentions and feelings. Be that as it may, what is certain is that members of all known societies take it for granted that they are recognizable primarily by their faces – supplemented by mention of their names – as particular, unique people by all acquaintances in their group. This shows unequivocally how indissolubly the awareness of our own recognizability as distinct *from* other people is bound up with our awareness of our recognizability by other people. Only because people live in society with other people can they perceive themselves as individuals different from other people. And this self-perception as a person distinct from others cannot be separated from the awareness that one is also perceived by other people, not only as a person like them, but as in some respects different from all other people.[6]

VIII

The nature and degree of self-detachment change in the course of social development. I should like to suggest that one way to track down changes in the position of individual people within their societies, and the changes in self-perception that go hand in hand with social changes, would be to investigate the development of languages, and especially the way in which pronoun functions are symbolically represented at different stages of language development. When, in a medieval French epic, the palace gatekeeper sometimes still says "thou" and sometimes already "you", one might suppose that the splitting of the form of address between a "thou" and a "you" is the symbolic representation of an increasing social distance. When, in a peasant's letter from the past, the words "we" and "us" appear more often than "I" and "me" – or, more exactly, more often than one would expect of an urban letter-writer of that time – one can assume that the balance of we- and I-identity tilted more to the side of we-identity in the case of the peasant, and more towards I-identity in that of the urban correspondent.

Since the European Middle Ages the balance between we- and I-identity has undergone a noticeable change, that can be characterized briefly as follows: earlier the balance of we- and I-identity was heavily weighted towards the former. From the Renaissance on the balance tilted more and more towards I-identity. More and more frequent became the cases of people whose we-identity was so weakened that they appeared to themselves as we-less I's. Whereas previously people had belonged, whether from birth or from a certain point in their lives, to a certain group for ever, so that their I-identity was permanently bound to their we-identity and often overshadowed by it, in the course of time the pendulum swung to the opposite extreme. The we-identity of people, though it certainly always remained present, was now often overshadowed or concealed in consciousness by their I-identity.

When Descartes wrote his famous sentence *Cogito*, *ergo sum*, he was the pioneer of a growing shift of emphasis in the human self-image, a shift from the then established overlaying of the I-identity by we-identity to the converse. At Descartes's time most members of a society were still permanently assigned, often by heredity, i.e. their family origin, to a certain group. The princes, kings and emperors, as individuals, owed their high position in society, and the wealth that went with it, to their birth as members of a family privileged by heredity, a dynasty. In the same way nobles, considered as individuals, owed their positions to the family into which they were born. Their identification with their ancestral groups, as shown in their family trees, largely determined their individual identity. Citizens belonged to guilds, which also often had an hereditary character. The peasants, the great majority of the population, were tied to the land. An exception was formed by members of the church. They were not hereditarily bound to the church when they made their vows, but only for life, i.e. individually. Naturally, there were always individuals who withdrew from their group bond and wandered the world, like the itinerant scholars, as groupless persons. But in a society where group membership – often hereditary – had decisive importance for an individual's position and prospects, groupless people had less scope to rise in society. The humanists were one of the earliest groups of people whose personal achievements and character traits gave them opportunities to rise to respected social positions, particularly as state and municipal officials. The shift towards individualization that they represented was certainly a sign of a change in the social structure.

Descartes's *Cogito*, with its accent on the I, was also a sign of this change in the position of the individual person in his society. While thinking, Descartes could forget all the we-relations of his person. He could forget that he had acquired a French mother tongue and Latin as the language of educated people, that every thought he formulated, including his *Cogito, ergo sum*, was conditioned by a linguistic tradition that had been learned, and not least that he was encoding his ideas somewhat for fear of the ever-alert church Inquisition. While working on the *Meditations* he heard of Galileo's arrest. While thinking he forgot that he was communicating with other people. He forgot other people in their role as we, you or they. They were *de facto* always present in the philosopher's consciousness as he sent his triumphant "I" out into the world. But the group he belonged to, the society to which he owed his language and knowledge, disappeared as he thought. In his consciousness the isolated I stepped out of the shadow of social allegiances, and the we–I pendulum swung in the opposite direction. The isolated thinker perceived himself – or more precisely, his own thought, his "reason" – as the only real, indubitable thing. All else might possibly be an illusion conjured up by the Devil, but not this, not his own existence as thinker. This form of I-identity, the perception of one's own person as a we-less I, has spread wide and deep since then.

A great part of the philosophical theory of knowledge – one might say the whole tradition of its classical representatives from Descartes through Berkeley and his thesis *Esse est percipi* (to be is to be perceived) or Kant, who found it impossible to say that objects of the outer world were not within the subject himself, to Husserl's wrestling with solipsism – rests on the idea that the human being who tries to acquire knowledge is an isolated being who must remain for ever in doubt whether objects, and there-fore persons, actually exist outside himself.[7] If it were just a matter of a single person who felt like a totally isolated being and was plagued by constant doubt whether anything or anyone existed outside himself, one might perhaps diagnose this as a somewhat eccentric mental state, a kind of sickness. But the situation is that from the early modern period – especially but doubtless not only in philosophical writing – this basic problem shows an extraordinary persistence transcending individual per-sons over a number of centuries. It is the problem of the person who perceives himself as standing totally alone and who cannot resist doubting the existence of anything or anyone outside himself. A whole flood of writings from the second half of the twentieth century presents the reading public with one version after another of the same basic figure of the isolated person, in the form of the *homo clausus* or the we-less I, in his voluntary or involuntary loneliness. And the wide resonance achieved by such writings, the lasting nature of their success, shows that the image of the isolated human being and the fundamental experience that gives him his strength, is not an isolated phenomenon.

There are passages in Sartre's well-known novel *Nausea* of which one could almost say that Descartes has been resurrected. But in Descartes the individual's doubt of the existence of the outside world and the idea that doubt, i.e. thinking, was the only guarantee of his own existence, were something new. The joy of discovery and the whole climate of rising modernity in France and especially in the Netherlands, where Descartes had found a second home, counteracted the possibility that the doubt might lead to despair. And the verb *esse* took on a new gravity through being transformed into the verb "to exist", and often enough gained an existence of its own, a reification, through the philosophical use of the associated noun "existence":

> . . . this sort of painful rumination: *I exist*, I am the one who keeps it up. I. The body lives by itself once it has begun. But thought – *I* am the one who continues it, unrolls it. I exist. How serpentine is this feeling of existing – I unwind it, slowly . . . If I could keep myself from thinking! I try, and succeed: my head seems to fill with smoke . . . and then it starts again: "Smoke . . . not to think . . . don't want to think . . . I think I don't want to think. I mustn't think that I don't want to think. Because that's still a thought." Will there never be an end to it?
>
> My thought is *me:* that's why I can't stop. I exist because I think . . . and I can't stop myself from thinking.[8]

We find another example of a we-less or almost we-less I in Camus's *The Outsider*. One of the peculiarities of the lonely man that the hero of this book appears to be is a curious confusion of the emotions. He kills someone, but the corresponding feelings, whether of hate or remorse, are lacking. His mother dies, but he feels, actually, nothing. The feelings of grief or being left behind alone do not arise. Isolation, abandonment are the permanent underlying feelings. They are not associated with people. The I is alone, without any real relation to other people, without the feelings that the we-relation makes possible. This theme occurs again and again in literature, and each time it strikes a chord. To give only one other example, there is the almost we-less hero of a novel entitled *La Salle de bain*. Throughout the book the hero repeatedly withdraws from other people into the bathroom. When his girlfriend asks him why he has left the capital and her, he cannot answer. He suffers from solitude, but does not know why he is alone. He suffers, and thinks suffering the last proof that he exists: "La souffrance était l'ultime assurance de mon existence, la seule."[9] Suffering, he withdraws constantly to the bathroom. What is he suffering from?

The we-less I that Descartes presents to us as the subject of knowledge already feels to a certain extent imprisoned in his own thought, in what one could reifyingly call his "reason". Seen positively, one's own thought becomes the only thing in the world that is indubitable. For Berkeley one's own senses form the walls of the prison; the sense perceptions of the isolated person are all that one can experience of other people and other things. One cannot doubt that in all these examples we have to do with an authentic experience, a genuine mode of self-perception. The elaboration of this self-perception in the form of a theory of knowledge omits, in a curious way which is repeated with great regularity, to take account of the fact that each adult has as a child to acquire knowledge from others in a long learning process, before he or she is able to develop this knowledge individually. The philosophical image of man as a static being who exists as an adult without ever having been a child, the omission of the process in which each person is constantly engaged, is one of the reasons for the dead-end that epistemology constantly comes up against.

Another reason is a forgetting of the constant meetings of the individual with other people and the intermeshing of his life with those of others in the course of this process. That a feeling of we-lessness is one of the basic problems of this specific image of man is seen particularly clearly in the literary examples from recent times. In them we come upon a peculiar conflict of human beings that, we can be sure, is not confined to literature. The experience underlying the notion of the we-less I is clearly the conflict between the natural human need for an emotive affirmation of one's own person by others and others' need of affirmation by oneself, on one hand, and fear of fulfilment of the need and resistance to it on the other. The need to love and be loved is, to an extent, the strongest condensation of this natural human craving. It can also take the form of the giving and finding of friendship. Whatever form it takes, the emotive need for human society, a giving and receiving in affective relationships to other people, is one of the fundamental conditions of human existence. What the bearers of the human image of the we-less I appear to suffer from is the conflict between the desire for emotional relationships with other people and their own inability to satisfy this desire. The heroes of the stories mentioned are alone because a personal sorrow denies them the possibility of genuine feelings for other people, genuine emotional bonds. The chord struck by this theme, particularly in the twentieth century, suggests that we are not concerned here with an isolated, individual problem, but with a habitus problem, a basic feature of the social personality structure of people in the modern age.

These brief indications may be enough to throw the dominant direction of the sequence of stages in the development of the we–I balance into somewhat sharper relief. At the earlier stages, as I have said, the we–I balance first tilted strongly towards the we. In more recent times it has often swung strongly towards the I. The question is whether the development of humanity, or the all-embracing form of human communal life, has already reached a stage, or can ever reach a stage, when a more stable equilibrium of the we–I balance will prevail.

IX

The complexity of humanity at its present stage of development makes it necessary at this point to take a further step forward in our thought. When we speak of a we–I balance, it may seem at first sight as if there were only one level or plane of integration in relation to which people can say "we". In the past, and certainly in the Stone Age, when people combined in very small groups preoccupied with seeking food as hunter-gatherers, there was indeed a stage when human societies had only a single plane of integration. Every linguistic expression with the same function as the word "we", even in the form of a proper name, had only one layer. In the present structure of human society, by contrast, the expression "we", and so, too, the social habitus of individuals in a wider sense, has many layers. The usefulness of the concept of the we–I balance as a tool of observation and reflection may perhaps be enhanced if we pay some attention to this multi-layered aspect of we-concepts. It matches the plurality of inter-locking integration planes characteristic of human society at its present stage of development.

It is to give a mere selection of the possible we-relations to point out that people can say "we" in relation to their families or friends, to villages or towns where they live, to nation states, to post-national units combining several nation states and finally in relation to mankind. One readily sees that the intensity of identi-fication varies widely with these different integration planes. The involvement or commitment expressed by the use of the pronoun "we" is probably usually strongest in relation to family, domicile or native region, and affiliation to a nation state. The emotional tinge of we-identity grows noticeably fainter in relation to post-national forms of integration, such as unions of African, Latin

American, Asian or European states. The function of the highest plane of integration, humanity, as a focus of human we-identity may be growing. But it is probably not an exaggeration to say that for most people mankind as a frame of reference for we-identity is a blank area on their emotional maps.

In enquiring into the reasons for the different emotional charge at different levels of integration, it is useful to bear in mind that the charges are variable. The family as a frame of reference for we-identity no doubt remains a human grouping which, for good or ill, commands a fairly high emotive charge in its members. But the tone of this feeling has changed markedly in connection with a profound structural change in the relation of the individual to every kind of social grouping, but particularly in the case of the family. At earlier stages of social development the relation to what we now call the family, i.e. to the larger or smaller association of relatives, was completely inescapable for most individuals. For a long time people belonged to their families for better or worse. This bond was only alterable in the case of the generally less powerful sex, women, through marriage. The strength of family ties had much to do with the very extensive function of the family or, as the case may be, the clan, as a survival unit. The decisive change which occurred in we-identity and in the corresponding emotional orientation towards the family is largely due to the fact that the family is no longer inescapable as a we-group. From a certain age, the individual can usually withdraw from the family without forfeiting his or her chances of physical or social survival.

This greater frequency of non-permanent or, at least, potentially changeable relations between individual people is, one might perhaps say, one of the structural features of modern state societies, considered more generally, in which the advance of individualization bound up with the rise of these societies has played an influential part. Often in combination with a reduction in the power differential (not to be confused with equality of power), the greater variability of relationships forces individuals to take a kind of repeated inventory, a test of relations which is at the same time a test of themselves. They have to ask themselves more often: how do we stand in relation to each other? As the forms of relationship across the whole spectrum, including those between men and women and children and parents, are comparatively variable, or at least not inescapable, their exact form is increasingly the responsibility of the individual partners.

The greater impermanence of we-relationships, which at earlier stages often had the lifelong, inescapable character of an external constraint, puts all the more emphasis on the I, one's own person, as the only permanent factor, the only person with whom one must live one's whole life. If we review the various levels of integration, we see this clearly. Many family relationships, which earlier were obligatory, lifelong, external constraints for many people, now increasingly have the character of a voluntary, revocable union which places higher demands on the capacity for self-regulation of the people concerned, and equally for both sexes. Changes in professional relationships are tending in the same direction; many paid professional activities have become interchangeable in more developed societies.[10] Even nationality has become exchangeable within limits. This whole development contributes towards a tilting of the I–we balance towards the I in the more developed countries.[11] The individual now has to rely far more on himself or herself in deciding on the form of relationships, whether to continue or end them. In conjunction with the reduced permanence, a greater interchangeability of relationships, a peculiar form of social habitus has emerged. This structure of relationships demands of the individual a greater circumspection, more conscious forms of self-control, reduced spontaneity in action and speech in the forming and management of relationships.

But this social moulding of human relationships has not extinguished the basic human need for impulsive warmth and spontaneity in relationships with other people. It has not caused the desire for security and constancy in the emotive affirmation of one's own person by others, and its counterpart, the desire for the company of people one likes, to disappear. The advanced social differentiation that goes hand in hand with an equally advanced differentness between people, or individualization, brings with it a great diversity and variability of personal relationships. One variety of them which often occurs is marked by the basic conflict of the we-less I which was mentioned earlier: a desire for emotional warmth, for affective affirmation of other people and by other people, coupled to an inability to give spontaneous emotional warmth. In such cases the habit of circumspection in forming relationships has not stifled the desire to give and receive emotional warmth and for commitment in relations to others, but it has stifled the ability to give or receive them oneself. In such cases people are not equal to the demands made on them by a strong emotional affirmation by another person. They seek and desire that affirmation, but have lost the capacity to respond with the same spontaneity and warmth when they meet it.

What emerges is this: the advance of individualization, which can be observed in phenomena such as changes in the kin group and thus in the family in the narrower sense, has, in some ways, a paradigmatic character. This is better understood if it is recalled that at earlier stages the family group was the primary, indispensable survival unit for individuals. It has not quite lost this function, especially for children. But in more recent times the state – and most recently the parliamentary state with certain, minimal welfare institutions – has absorbed this function of the family like many others. First in the form of the absolutist state, then in the form of the one- or multi-party state, the state level of integration has, for more and more people, taken over the role of the primary survival unit, a role that seems indispensable and permanent.

X

It may be worthwhile to look somewhat more closely at the fact that at present, among the groups to which the we-identity of individuals relates, societies organized as states[12] are given special importance. We lack the space here to enquire in more detail why this is the case. The short, obvious answer is that states, more than any other social form, have emerged all over the world as the highest-ranking survival units. For thousands of years, indeed as long as societies in state form have existed, states have shared the function of survival unit with societies organized in pre-state forms, such as clans or tribes. In Roman-Greek anti-quity and as late as the early modern period, tribes sometimes posed a serious threat to states. At present, the age of the autonomous tribe is coming to an end all over the world. Every-where they are relinquishing to states their role as independent survival units and as the highest-ranking reference groups for the we-identity of individuals.

It may be that the nation-state-based we-identity of the indi-vidual in our day is almost taken for granted. One does not always remember clearly enough that the role of the state as a frame of reference for the we-identity of the great majority of all members of a state, i.e. the state's role as nation state, is of relatively recent date.

The emergence of the European states as we-units happened gradually and in stages. What above all distinguishes the earlier stage of the absolutist state from the multi-party state is the fact that the princes ruling the former, thanks to a very great power differential between rulers and ruled, could regard the whole state organization, including the population, as a kind of personal property. They said "we" not in relation to the population but to themselves. The dictum ascribed to Louis XIV, "I am the state", shows a specific fusion of "we" and "I" in relation to the dynasty and the incumbent of the throne, and only to them. The popula-tion, for their part, perceived the autocratic princely state to only a low degree as a layer of their we-groups, and very much as a grouping to be spoken and thought of in the third person, as "they", not "we". The princes and nobles, we can say, saw the state largely as their own state, as a we-unit confined to them-selves, and the mass of the population as people with whom they did not identify themselves. They alone, as the established group, formed the state. The mass of the population were perceived only as "they" and as outsiders. Even in the late nineteenth and early twentieth centuries parts of the population, first the peasants, then the industrial proletariat, were excluded from the citizens' we-identity by the ruling classes, the bourgeoisie and nobility. And these outsiders did not cease to perceive the state as something of which one said "they", hardly "we".

A synthesis from a high viewpoint shows a peculiar picture – a series of conflicts between established and outsider groups rising like steps from a broader and broader basis, conflicts which sooner or later, usually in conjunction with wars, led to a more or less limited integration of the earlier outsider group into the nation-state society. In the absolutist states princes and nobles were the only established group, although higher bourgeois officials attained a position as a second-rank established group. Then the previously excluded bourgeois groups gained control of state monopolies. They were followed, with more or less restricted access to the key state monopolies, by the previous outsider group of industrial workers, whose rise also played a considerable part in the development of the state welfare organization. At present the bourgeois and worker strata as the established we-group together confront a new wave of immigrant outsiders who perform low-paid menial tasks. As at the earlier stages, the outsiders are not included in the we-identity. Here too the established groups perceive the outsiders as a third-person group. One should add, however, that these insider–outsider conflicts have a somewhat different character in the old European states from the one we find in countries like the United States of America, which have a tradition of limited assimilation of outsider groups.

Perhaps a glance at the acute problems between established and outsider groups in the late twentieth century helps us to understand the integration problems of previous phases of development. The more complete integration of all citizens into the state in the European multi-party states has really only happened in the course of the twentieth century. Only in conjunction with the parliamentary representation of all classes did all the members of the state begin to perceive it more as a we-unit and less as a they-group. Only in the course of the two great wars of this century did the populations of the more developed industrial states take on the character of nations in the more modern sense of the word, and their states the character of nation states. Nation states, one might say, are born in wars and for wars. Here we find the explanation why, among the various layers of we-identity, the state level of integration today carries special weight and a special emotional charge. The integration plane of the state, more than any other layer of we-identity, has in the consciousness of most members the function of a survival unit, a protection unit on which depends their physical and social security in the conflicts of human groups and in cases of physical catastrophe.

We should note, however, that it has this function only in the *consciousness* of most of its members. How things stand in reality is quite a different matter. Of course, the integration plane of a state is, in some respects, a survival unit. One of the state's functions is to protect the individual as a subject from the violence of other people within and outside the state territory. But states threaten each other. In their efforts to guarantee the physical and social security of their citizens in face of possible attack by other states, they continually give the impression that they threaten those by whom they feel threatened. The constant switching of roles that turns threatened states into threatening ones, also turns the hoped-for survival units unintentionally into potential or actual annihilation units. This is true not only for members of opposed states, but for members of one's own. The specifically two-edged nature of the national credo derives not least from the fact that the state's function as survival unit, as guarantor of its members' security, is combined with the demand that its members be prepared to forfeit their own lives should the government deem this necessary for the security of the whole nation. In the name of lasting security the leading men and women of the nation states, particularly the most powerful ones, create a state of permanent insecurity.

The peculiar dichotomy of nation states as survival units and annihilation units is, of course, nothing new. Nation states share this functional contradiction with the kin groups of earlier times, with the tribal units of past and present, to name only these. But in our day, in view of the evolution of armaments, the danger that the nation's efforts to secure its survival may produce the opposite result is greater than ever before.

Moreover, the dual function of contemporary nation states as survival units and as potential or actual annihilation units finds expression in peculiarities of the social habitus of the individuals forming these states. I said earlier that in the course of the recent development of humanity, at least in the more developed societies, I-identity, as compared to we-identity, has taken on a stronger emotive charge in the I–we balance of individuals. Especially in the human image of philosophers – and of quite a number of sociologists – the extreme notion of a we-less I plays a highly prominent part. But this weakening of we-identity is by no means evenly spread across the whole spectrum of we-layers. Powerful as the advance of individualization has been in recent times, in relation to the nation-state plane we-identity has actually strengthened. One often finds that people try to overcome the contradiction between their self-perception as a we-less I, as a totally isolated individual, and their emotional involvement in the we-group of the nation by a strategy of encapsulation. Their self-perceptions as an individual and as a representative of a we-group, as a Frenchman, Englishman, West German, American, etc., are assigned to different compartments of their knowledge, and these compartments communicate only very tenuously with each other. Looking more closely one finds that the traits of national group identity – what we call the "national character" – are a layer of the social habitus built very deeply and firmly into the personality structure of the individual.

The social habitus, and therefore the layer of habitus forming the national character, is certainly not an enigma. As a social formation it is, like language, both hard and tough, but also flexible and far from immutable. It is, in fact, always in flux.

A closer investigation of the educational processes that play a decisive part in the formation of the I- and we-images of young people would readily throw more light on the production and reproduction of I- and we-identity over generations. It could show how the changing power relationships, both within and between states, influence the formation of feelings in this area. In fact, the manipulation of feelings in relation to state and nation, government and political system, is a widespread technique in social praxis. In all nation states the institutions of public education are dedicated to an extreme degree to deepening and consolidating a we-feeling based exclusively on the national tradition. This whole area still lacks a factual and practical social theory which would enable us to understand such matters and would thus help to overcome the idea of a separate existence of individual and society.

The concept of social habitus is not yet part of the basic stock of theoretical knowledge which teachers of sociology and the other social sciences impart to the younger generation in giving them a perspective on human society. The deeply rooted nature of the distinctive national characteristics and the consciousness of national we-identity closely bound up with them can serve as a graphic example of the degree to which the social habitus of the individual provides a soil in which personal, individual differences can flourish. The individuality of the particular Englishman, Dutchman, Swede or German represents, in a sense, the personal elaboration of a common social, and in this case national, habitus.

A process-sociological study, and a familiarity with the investigation of long-term processes, are needed to explain the differences of individual habitus in Latin America or Europe, Africa or Asia. But if we are looking for examples of the reality-congruence of the habitus concept, we could hardly find a more cogent example than the persistent way in which the national habitus of the European nation states impedes their closer political union.

XI

We encounter here a problem of social development that may still be somewhat underestimated on both the theoretical-empirical and the practical level. To simplify communication I shall call it the drag effect. It is a habitus problem of a peculiar kind.

In studying social development processes we repeatedly come across a constellation in which the dynamic of unplanned social processes is tending to advance beyond a given stage towards another, which may be higher or lower, while the people affected by this change cling to the earlier stage in their personality structure, their social habitus. It depends entirely on the relative strength of the social shift and the deep-rootedness and therefore the resistance of the social habitus whether – and how quickly – the dynamic of the unplanned social process brings about a more or less radical restructuring of this habitus, or whether the social habitus of individuals successfully opposes the social dynamic, either by slowing it down or blocking it entirely.

There are many examples of such drag effects. The barrier just mentioned which the national habitus of the members of European states puts in the way of the formation of a European continental state is only one. The tensions and conflicts associated with it may be made easier to understand by looking from a greater distance to analogous events at an earlier stage of development, that of the transition from tribes to states as the dominant units of survival and integration. A typical situation in this respect is the one which once confronted the North American Indians and probably still confronts them.

One has the impression that the solidity, the resistance, the deep-rootedness of the social habitus of individauls in a survival unit is greater the longer and more continuous the chain of generations within which a certain social habitus has been transmitted from parents to children. Before the advent of the Europeans the dominant men in many Indian tribes bore, as far as we can see now, the social stamp of warriors and hunters.

The women were gatherers and helped in many ways with the central occupation of the warriors and hunters. The primordial survival unit, the highest level of we-identity, was the tribe. At this early stage of development it played a similar role to the nation state at a later one. The personal identification of the individual with a tribe was therefore as natural as it was necessary. To it as the highest we-unit and source of meaning, in other words, was attuned the social habitus, the social character or the social personality structure of the individual.

But then social reality changed. In a long series of wars and other forms of power struggle the descendants of the European immigrants became the rulers of the land. They built up a social organization on the more complex integration level of the state. The Indians formed islands with an earlier, pre-state form of organization which continued to exist like a semi-petrified formation, like fossils amid the developing American state society. Almost all the natural and social conditions that had shaped their social structure had long disappeared, but in the social habitus of individuals, in their personality structure, the vanished social structure survived and, aided by the pressure of public opinion within the tribe and by education, was transmitted from generation to generation. The result was the fossilization of the social habitus of these people within their island reserves.

This constellation, the preservation of the traditional we-identity in museum-like reserves, is one of the possible outcomes of the drag effect. Fragments of the traditional habitus and customs survive, if only as tourist attractions. But the social form which gave the habitus and customs their social function, particularly the life of warriors and hunters, disappeared with the embedding of the tribe in a large nation state. There are alternatives. To mention only one: in some cases American Indians have successfully transformed themselves into industrial workers. The traditional social habitus gives way. The assimilation of the Indians into the state within which they live has begun.

The drag effect is no less detectable in the case of the African tribes who are combining into states before our eyes, partly in the course of violent struggles for supremacy and partly through more or less peaceful integration. In Africa south of the Sahara one can observe how many variants the social process of transition from the tribal level of integration to that of the state admits. In a large number of cases, as in Ghana and Nigeria, the process of tribal merging began in the colonial period, and in Nigeria a bitter war put an end to the aspiration of one tribe to exist within a state of its own. In Tanzania a charismatic leader used his authority at great cost to dismantle the tribes, trying to weld the uprooted units together again under the banner of African socialism. In Uganda a long period of bloody struggle for tribal supremacy may be coming to an end. For the first time the representative of one of the tribal groups is fighting successfully, as the advocate of a state-related we-identity, against the proponents of tribe-related we-identity. Despite all the differences, the basic structure is always the same. The dynamic of the unplanned social process, which urges tribes to combine in the wider integration unit of the state, is almost inescapable. But the social habitus of people is in most cases just as inescapably tailored to integration and we-identity in the form of a tribe. The example of the state formation processes now going on in Africa shows with special clarity both the strength of the social process urging people towards integration on the state plane, and their resistance to this integration, which owes its strength and persistence to the attunement of the social habitus to the traditional tribal plane.

As a phase of an unplanned social process the current shift towards integration is far too powerful to be held up for long by particular social units, still less individuals. But at the tribal level (as at the nation state level) it brings specific conflicts with it. They do not happen by chance. They are part of the structure of the whole process. Such process-conflicts are partly bound up with the change in the social personality structure of the individual members of groups, a change enforced by the change from one integration level to another, e.g. from the tribal to the state level. Some conflicts of this type have to be fought out by the

individual with himself. They can take the form of a conflict
between loyalty to the family and to the state, as in the case of the
so-called "corruption" in less developed states mentioned earlier.
In other constellations they take the form of a conflict of
generations.[13] But they always indicate that, as compared to the
relatively rapid change of the integration shift, the pace of the
corresponding change in the social habitus of the individuals
concerned is extraordinarily slow. The social personality structures of individuals, including I- and we-images, are relatively
durable. They oppose all the manifold innovations that the transition to a new integration level entails. In the case of the transition
from tribe to state the pressure of development is, as we have
said, so immense that resistance in the name of the tribe cannot
succeed in the long run. But it usually takes at least three
generations for these process-conflicts to die down. And as these
transitions are attended not only by the personal conflicts of
individuals or even generation conflicts, but always by power
struggles between different tribes, it can take much longer than
three generations for the transitional conflicts to be resolved and
for the relative positions of different tribes within the new state
formation to attain a certain stability.

XII

The dominant pressure urging people towards state integration
now usually leaves the pre-state units, e.g. tribes, only the choice
between preserving their identity as a kind of museum piece, a
stagnant backwater on the periphery of a rapidly developing
humanity, or renouncing a part of their identity and therefore the
traditional social habitus of their members. This may happen
either by integrating themselves into a pre-existing unit on the
level of a nation state or continental state, or by combining with
other tribes into a new nation state. In a few special cases,
however, there is a third alternative: the encapsulation of an
older, pre-state society within a large state society which is so

powerful and self-confident that it can tolerate such encapsulated earlier societies in its midst.

The North American state societies offer a large number of examples of this kind of social encapsulation, of societies surviving from a pre-state stage of development within a more highly developed state society. Some representatives of a pre-state society which survive embedded in a state society while preserving a good part of their pre-state form, are able to do so because they can fulfil certain functions within the dominant state society. In Canada, for example, there are very successful settlements of old Christian sects which are able to maintain their forms of life, their religion and their whole tradition in a petrified form because the work ethos and power structure of their pre-state stage of development allow them to grow agricultural produce competitively, and to find willing buyers in the surrounding society. The sect of German Hutterer[14] in Canada is one example. Their internal social life is at a standstill. They wear the costume of their forefathers; they speak their language. The we–I balance, as in many other pre-state groups, is weighted heavily in favour of the we. Television, radio, telephone contact with the outside world and other media that would counteract the encapsulation are lacking. The simple dress, the same for all men and for all women, gives hardly any scope for individualization. The high birth-rate allows new villages to be established. A council of elders sees to it that the tradition remains intact. The children are brought up with a combination of strictness and kindness to fit into this life.

Another example of a pre-state social form surviving within the framework of a state form is the American Mafia. Its tradition dates from a time when the kin group functioned as the main survival unit for the individual. In its country of origin, Sicily, the extended family groups of the Mafia have kept a higher survival value than the Italian state up to the present. They owe this function largely to the unconditional, lifelong loyalty of individual members to the extended family group, actual or nominal. In the form of the Mafia, a kind of configuration that was widespread at an earlier stage of development obtrudes into the present stage in a suitably adapted form, now under negative auspices. In this case the kin group has retained a high survival function for its members, even in comparison to the state unit and despite the latter's claim to a monopoly in the use of violence and taxation.

The family associations of the Mafia have also very successfully opposed this monopoly claim in the United States. Taking root there too, they have found a way of continuing to exist as representatives of a specific group tradition by taking over social functions which run counter to state law. The Mafia families have changed in the United States too into a criminal formation which, by organizing the drug traffic, gambling, prostitution and the illegal exercise of violence, has taken up an outsider position which up to now has at times been very successful. One of the basic conditions of their survival has been the fact that certain pre-state forms of communal life have maintained in them an illegal, anti-state, twilight existence – particularly in large cities. This is true above all of the loyalty already mentioned which an individual has to his "family", that is, to a we–I balance in favour of we, which has been unusual in more developed states. What has contributed much to the Mafia's success has been, in other words, certain structural features of the pre-state kin association, such as is found in its original form – usually designated as "feudal" in the technical language – only in predominantly agrarian societies. They reappear in a less structured form in keeping with the urban and state conditions and as a result of being forced into criminality.

Most important among the configurational features which these encapsulated forms of pre-state groups within the body of contemporary large states have in common, as has become clear here, is the greater, often lifelong permanence of many human relationships, if not all, and a we–I balance in which the we has clear preponderance over the I and which often demands the unconditional subordination of the I to the we, of the individual to the we-group. If one sees this structural feature, as it were, *in vivo* while having conceptual tools to hand that allow comparisons, one can perhaps understand more easily that the tilting of the we–I balance in favour of the I is not something to be simply taken for granted, still less a fact of human nature. Underlying it, too, is a particular form of communal life; it too is characteristic of a specific social structure. The present form of individualization, the prevailing appearance of the we–I image, is no less conditioned by the social standard of the civilizing process and the corresponding process of individual civilization, than these pre-state forms of social habitus.

It is, perhaps, necessary to say that what is at issue in this endeavour to elaborate the particular structures of the social habitus of individuals and, especially, of the we–I balance at various stages of development, is not the question which form of this balance or of the social habitus one personally prefers. We can take it almost for granted that someone who has grown up at a later stage of development, at the present one, prefers the more I-weighted self-image of our own time, and that the more we-weighted self-image of pre-state societies will appear alien to him or her. What such observations and reflections bring to light is the fact that the we- and I-identity of the individual person is neither so self-evident nor so immutable as it may seem at first sight, before these problems are brought within the field of sociological investigation, both theoretical and empirical.

XIII

It is a peculiarity of the twentieth century that in its course integration shifts have taken place not just on one plane but on several simultaneously. On one hand humanity, usually without directly intending to, has in some regions of the world attained a stage of development which, in terms of all the sources of power – technical, military, economic and so on – lies far beyond the area within which nominally independent tribes, or even kin groups, are really able to maintain their independence, their competitiveness or their function as survival units. On the other hand, however, the function of the effective survival unit is now visibly shifting more and more from the level of the nation states to the post-national unions of states and, beyond them, to humanity. The catastrophe of Chernobyl, the large-scale destruction of fish and the pollution of the Rhine after the disorganized attempt to combat a fire in a Swiss chemical works, can serve as limited but instructive examples of the fact that nation state units have in reality already relinquished their function as guarantors of the physical security of their citizens, and thus as survival units, to supra-state units.

The representatives of European states are very familiar with the meaning of power balances and power shifts in the relations between states. But the incumbents of the leading positions, above all political and military, in the present states are often so inundated with short-term problems that they are seldom in a position to harmonize their plans and actions seriously with long-term developmental trends. During and shortly after the Second World War states of a new order of magnitude, sometimes called superpowers today, i.e. the United States and the Soviet Union above all, moved to the top of the hierarchy of states, pushing the smaller European states with more limited military and economic resources, particularly Great Britain and France, into a second-rank position. The speed with which this change of scene in the network of states took place clearly took most European states-men and military commanders by surprise, as well, no doubt, as most other people. If the scientific investigation of long-term configurative changes, and thus of long-term changes in the balance of power between states, had been at a more advanced stage, this alteration in the hierarchy of states could have been foreseen without difficulty as a not improbable, if not a necessary, accompaniment to the defeat of Hitler. In the same way it can be predicted as probable if not necessary that in the course of the next century a further shift in the balance of power to the disadvantage of the individual European states and in favour of other states and groups of states with greater military and economic potential will take place. The competitive pressure of non-European states on the individual nation states of Europe, which is already visible enough in the case of Japan, will probably intensify in all areas, including, for example, the scientific and cultural areas.

There are several long-term strategies that one could decide on as a response to this problem. One of them is a closer union with and greater dependence on the United States. Another is a gradually increasing union of European states in the form of a multilingual federation of states or a federal state. A third possibility is the continued existence of European states more or less in their traditional form, as nation states each of which is nominally independent and sovereign.

The third of these possibilities demands special attention in this context, since the continued existence of European nation states as formally independent survival units best matches the social habitus of the people belonging to them. States such as Great Britain, the Netherlands, Denmark or France have developed continuously as relatively autonomous organizational units over several centuries, and in the past century in particular there has been a strong advance of functional democratization, integrating practically all classes into the state structure. These developments have brought about a deep-rooted predisposition of the individual personality structures of people of all classes to live together in this specific form, as Danes, Dutch or French. The common language in itself binds the individual strongly to the state in its traditional form. Something similar is true of the way people are attuned to competition within the state, or personal feeling to the familiar we-image and we-identity. The individual's emotional ties to his own state may be ambivalent; they often take a love–hate form. But whatever they may be like, the bond to one's own state is strong and vivid. It is comparatively pale, or non-existent, in relation to the preliminary forms of the European state federation. Here we come across a further, impressive example of what I have called the drag effect.

Undoubtedly, strategic and economic factors play an important part in the difficulties standing in the way of a closer integration of the European nation states. But these obstacles might possibly be overcome by compromise, particularly as the social reality of the development of states towards post-national units emphatically demonstrates the disadvantages of Europe's fragmentation into nation states of various sizes. Nevertheless, the differences of habitus between the people making up these different nation states and the deep national commitment of individuals combined with their we-identity as a nation state, bear a far greater responsibility for the difficulties obstructing the formation of a post-national structure than is usually realized in public discussions on integration. This difference of national habitus and the emotionally charged national we-identity cannot be set aside by compromise, by an act of will or by what is usually understood as rational means. Both factors are the precipitate of a very long process, the historical evolution of the various national groups, in the personality structures of their individual members. Their resistance, even in face of strong pressure towards post-national unions, is explained not least by the fact that in the past they had very real significance in terms of the state's function as a survival unit. The difficulty is that in the course of the twentieth century the integration level of the traditional European nation states has lost much of its survival function. But the precipitate of this function in the feelings and characters of the individuals involved, the so-called "national character", leads to an ossifying of human attitudes that remains initially quite unmoved by changes in social reality.

In other words, the social habitus pertaining to the nation state and the we-image and we-ideal associated with it have a meaning of their own. This gives them a durability which can prevent them from continuing to develop in step with social development towards a higher level of integration. Examples are plentiful. Many functional areas in the development of mankind in our day tend unambiguously towards the formation of supranational units even within Europe. But the we-image, the whole social habitus of individuals, is immovably tied by a strong affective charge to traditional group identity on the plane of the nation state. On the tribal plane, the we-identity of the North American Indians, in which the greatness of their common past, the buffalo hunts, the tribal wars and not least the tribe's function as the decisive survival unit are reflected, opposed development into a state. In the same way, the we-image and the we-ideal of the nation state, in which past wars and the by now obsolete survival function of the nation are reflected, stand in the way of a further integration that would have a far better chance of succeeding in the non-military competition between nations, and even in war would represent a somewhat more effective survival unit than the nation state. The discrepancy of development stage and power is undoubtedly far greater in the case of the Indian tribes in relation to the American state than in that of the European nation states in relation to a perhaps unattainable European federation. But the difficulties in the way of European union will remain inaccessible to analysis, particularly scientific analysis, as long as individuals are regarded merely as we-less I's, and the role of the we–I balance and of the we-ideal and we-identity in individual feeling and behaviour is misunderstood.

There is clearly a split in the situation of nation states at present. On one hand the survival of a nation state as a self-ruling and independent society, as a sovereign state, has an important function for the people living in it. This function is often taken for granted, and one can imagine it might be useful to breach this tacit acceptance and expose the function of membership of a nation for the people concerned to impartial public discussion. For there are, on the other hand, unquestionable structural features of the present stage of the development of mankind which run counter to national sovereignty and tend increasingly to curtail it. This fundamental split, and its far-reaching implications, are not at present the subject of much objective discussion. The split is regarded not as a fact but a matter of belief. It is not discussed as a factual problem, personal involvement being deliberately held in check, but in terms of quasi-religious slogans and emotive party doctrines which fix personal responses before the scientific discussion of the facts has begun. In this context it must be enough to point out that it is high time the problem of the evolution and function of the nation state was taken seriously as a problem for process-sociological investigation. This would involve analysing differences of nation state development in relation to the corresponding differences in the social personality structure of the people concerned.

The powerful shift towards integration affecting humanity in our time favours survival units which are superior to nation states in their number of levels of integration, territorial extent, size of population and thus of internal market, social capital, military potential and in many other respects. Survival units at the stage of development of nation states cannot compete with state organizations at the next stage, primarily the United States and the Soviet Union, without combining into larger, multinational states with greater resources. Developmental pressure, particularly technical and economic, and the whole pressure of international competition, is forcing human integration beyond the stage of nation states towards the formation of united states. But this pressure of unplanned development meets the opposing pressure of nation state we-identity, and up to now the latter has usually been stronger. Whereas, in the transition from tribe to state, the resistance of tribal traditions rooted in the social habitus of individuals has little chance of enforcing the survival of the independent tribe, the possibility that personality structures may successfully resist the pressure of integration is considerably greater in the transition from nation states to continental states or, at any rate, to post-national units.

XIV

The resistance to the merging of one's own survival unit with a larger unit – or its disappearance into that unit – is undoubtedly due in large part to a particular feeling. It is the feeling that the fading or disappearance of a tribe or state as an autonomous

entity would render meaningless everything which past generations had achieved and suffered in the framework and in the
name of this survival unit. Let us recall the enforced incorpora-
tion of the Indians into the United States. The disappearance of
cultural traditions during absorption into a larger unit does in fact
mean, in this and similar cases, a kind of collective dying. The
great deeds of the fathers and mothers who had risked their lives
for these traditions are forgotten. The mighty spirits and gods
who stood by the tribe in good times and bad are turned into
shadowy names which inspire neither fear nor hope. The ritual
implements, once saturated with feeling, turn into museum
curiosities for uncomprehending sightseers. This is in part a result
of the circumstance that on the tribal plane relatively few cultural
products of universal human significance are created. I say relatively few, for there are no doubt creations on this level which
have a value and meaning transcending the tribe. But they are
rare, and the incipient assimilation of Indian tribes to North
American urban society marks a break in tradition, a fading of
the Indians' group identity, a major fracture in the chain of
generations.

Something similar happens to states which are under pressure
to combine at a higher level. As with the tribe, something which
possesses high value for many of the people concerned, with
which they identify themselves, fades in the transition to the
higher level. The identity of their we-image is threatened. Such a
we-image, however, which often takes the form of a process of
greater or lesser length, has not only an individual function but an
important social one. It gives the individual person a past stretching far beyond his or her personal past, and it allows something of
the past people to live on in the present. Units like tribes and
states do not only have a survival function in the most obvious
sense of the word. They are not only survival units because the
people within them usually enjoy a relatively high level of physical security, protection from violence and succour in sickness and
old age, but because, by virtue of its continuous tradition, membership of this we-group grants the individual a chance of survival

beyond actual physical existence, survival in the memory of the
chain of generations. The continuity of a survival group, which
finds expression in the continuity of its language, the passing
down of legends, history, music and many other cultural values, is
itself one of the survival functions of such a group. The living on
of a past group in the memory of a present one has the function of
a collective memory. If a previously independent group gives up
its autonomy, whether through union with other units or by
assimilation to a more powerful one, this affects not only those
living at the time. Much that has happened in past generations,
that has lived on in the collective memory, in the we-image of the
group, changes or loses its meaning when the group's identity and
therefore its we-image change.

One can see the peculiar nature of the conflict which this brings
into focus. It is well known on the level of particular observations, as an event at a low level of synthesis: but we lack a
conception of it from a high level of synthesis. It is partly
concealed by the fact that the linguistic tradition offers convenient concepts which appear to resolve the problem at issue
satisfactorily but in fact bypass it. A pair of concepts that comes
readily to mind, for example, is "rational–irrational". It is simply
rational, one might say, to yield to the pressure of a powerful
integration process and irrational to resist it. But this pair of
concepts is itself an example of the drag effect I have referred to.
It comes from an earlier epoch in which people were clearly
pictured as beings who possessed a faculty of reason as if by
nature, and as a result were always able to act objectively. If they
did not do so they were being unreasonable, or irrational. There
was not room in this schema for feelings, whatever they might be
called – emotions, affects or human instincts. Nor was there room
for people who have an I- and we-image charged with feelings of
greater or lesser intensity. To leave people only the choice of
behaving rationally or irrationally is somewhat like treating them
as children who are either good or naughty. But in relation to
their own group identity and, more widely, their own social

habitus, people have no free choice. These things cannot be simply changed like clothes.

This also implies that the problem at issue cannot be conceptually resolved if it is treated as basically an intellectual matter, such as a question of values. The problem concerns the fixation of individual feeling and behaviour on a human association with important survival functions, even after this association has given up a good part of its functions to a higher level of integration. Seen as a purely intellectual problem, the absorption of one's own we-group into a we-group of a higher order appears merely as a devaluation of something highly prized. One might say that that is what it is. But it is far more than a devaluation. As long as no feelings of personal identity, no we-feelings are associated with the higher-order unit, the fading or disappearance of the lower-order we-group appears in reality as a kind of death threat, a collective destruction and certainly a loss of meaning to the highest degree. If resistance to integration at a higher level is presented as primarily a problem of thought, an intellectual problem, it can never be properly understood. For from an intellectual standpoint it is often quite clear that integration at a higher level in a world where other survival units at a higher level already exist is both unavoidable and advantageous. It would no doubt be appropriate and easy to understand intellectually if the American Sioux and Iroquois were to hang up their traditional costume, replace their customs with American customs and join into the highly individualized competition of American society. It would make rational sense and possibly bring benefits if the European nation states combined into the United States of Europe. But in most cases the difficulty lies in the fact that intellectual awareness of the logic of integration meets the tenacious resistance of emotive ideas which give the integration the character of ruin, a loss that one cannot cease mourning. And in such a situation, one probably does not want to cease mourning.

The central problem, as can perhaps be seen, lies in a peculiarity of the transition from one level of integration to another.

In the transitional period there is often a long phase when the group at the lower level suffers what its members feel to be a serious loss of the we-group meaning, while the group at the higher level is not yet able to take over the function of a we-group conferring emotive meaning. Think, for example, of the difference in emotional charge between the statements: "I am an Englishman", "I am a Frenchman", "I am a German", and the statement: 'I am an English, French or German European". All references to the individual European nation states have a strong emotive value to the people involved, whether positive, negative or ambivalent. Statements like "I am a European, a Latin American, an Asian" are emotively weak by comparison. The integration unit on the continental level may be understood to be a practical necessity, but unlike the older national units it is not associated with strong we-feelings. And yet it is not unrealistic to suppose that in the future terms like "European" or "Latin American" will take on a far stronger emotive content than they have at present.

XV

Nor is this all. Beside the two already discussed, the present advance of integration has a third level. On close examination we see clearly that the welfare or otherwise of the citizens of a single state, including the Soviet Union and the United States, no longer depends even in the present on the protection which this state – or even a potential continental state like Europe – can afford them. Even today the chances of survival depend largely on what happens on the global plane. It is the whole of mankind which now constitutes the last effective survival unit.

I spoke earlier of the increasing impermanence, interchangeability and voluntariness of many we-relationships, including, within certain limits, national status. Only the highest level of integration, membership of humanity, has remained permanent and inescapable. But our ties to this all-embracing we-unit are so loose that very few people, it seems, are aware of them as social bonds.

The actual course of social development in the past two decades has led to a constantly increasing interdependence of all human groups. The growing integration of mankind as not only the most comprehensive but as a highly effective integration plane shows itself in good ways and bad. The global intertwinement of all states expresses itself clearly enough in global central institutions at a very early stage of development. The United Nations is weak and in many ways ineffective. But anyone who has studied the growth of central institutions knows that integration processes which are precipitated in the setting up of central institutions at a new level often need a run-up period of several centuries before they are somewhat effective. And no one can foresee whether central institutions formed in the course of a powerful integration may not be destroyed in an equally powerful disintegration process. This applies not only to the United Nations but to other global institutions in their early forms, such as the World Bank, the World Health Organization, the Red Cross or Amnesty International. But the growing integration of humanity also expresses itself in malign ways: the struggle for global supremacy and the arms race between two hegemonic powers leading to a possible global war are some of its symptoms. Another, and not the least, is the technical possibility of the self-destruction of all mankind, or of the conditions for its survival, by developing weapons with ever greater destructive powers. In conjunction with the arms race this can be regarded as a realistic possibility for the first time in the development of mankind.

Among the curious features of the present situation is the fact that at this level too the we-image, the we-identity of most people lags behind the reality of the integration actually achieved. The we-image trails far behind the reality of global interdependence, which includes the possibility that the common living space will be destroyed by particular groups. The integration planes of the clan, the tribe or the state, as we have said, are positively or negatively charged with strong feelings of a common bond, with intense we-feelings which guide the actions of individuals in one direction or another. Union at higher levels, especially, now, the growing integration of mankind, may be understood as a fact; but as a focal point for feelings of belonging and as a guiding image for individual actions humanity is at a very early stage. The consciences of people, particularly the leading politicians, officers and businessmen throughout the world, are almost exclusively preoccupied with their own individual states. The sense of responsibility for imperilled humanity is minimal. Eminently realistic as such a concern may be, the habitus attuned to one's own nation makes it appear unrealistic, even naive. The broad, unplanned advance of integration does, to be sure, enforce alliances and multinational military organizations. But for the participants the single state is still pre-eminent as a reference point for we-considerations. The two leading powers, the Soviet Union and the United States, have such military preponderance that the half-truth of single-state sovereignty no longer really conceals the military dependence of their smaller allies. But the leaders of the two world powers, and therefore the military leaders, leave their allies in little doubt that the interests of their own state have precedence of all others in every respect.

The compulsion exerted by the social habitus attuned to the single state appears to many people today as so overwhelming and ineluctable that they take it for granted as something inherent in nature, like birth and death. They do not think about it. As a subject of research this habitus and its constraints largely lie fallow. They are part of the reality of social existence. The idea that they could change is regarded as naive. But the constraints of habitus are created by human beings. At one time in the past they were adjusted in all people to suit the integration level of the clan. At other stages in the past tribes were the highest integration units to which the human conscience and feelings were attuned. It is not so long ago that states became the integration units which attracted, if in an ambivalent form, especially strong we-feelings and imposed a relatively high obligation of loyalty and solidarity on all their members. The we-image of human beings has changed; it can change again. Such changes do not take place overnight. They involve processes that often take many generations. In the past the process of change has followed a particular direction. Larger social units took over the function of primary survival units from smaller ones. There is no necessity for the process to continue in the same direction. But it is not impossible. During the transition of the function of primary survival unit to social units representing a more comprehensive level of integration, discrepancies of the kind I encountered on various occasions in studying we–I relations have arisen with great regularity. Again and again a split has developed between the actual takeover of the primary survival function by social units at a higher stage of integration, and the persistent fixation of individuals' we-identity on units of an earlier stage.

Such discrepancies usually result in considerable behavioural malfunctions. At present, as I have said, social survival functions are shifting visibly from nation states of the European type to hegemonic states of the North American and Russian type, and now, more and more unambiguously, to mankind. Indeed, mankind is now emerging increasingly clearly as an effective integration level of the highest order. The corresponding development of the individual person's we-image lags far behind this integration, and, above all, we-feelings, the identification of human beings with human beings as such, regardless of their affiliation to a sub-group of mankind, is developing very slowly. One of the reasons for this is a unique peculiarity of humanity, considered as a single social unit. At all other levels of integration the we-feeling has developed in conjunction with threats to one's own group by other groups. Mankind itself, however, is not threatened by other, non-human groups, but only by sub-groups within itself. The actual effect, the possible destruction of mankind, is the same, whether the threat comes from within, from sections of humanity, or from outside, e.g. from the inhabitants of a different solar system. But the abolition of wars between human sub-groups and the engendering of a we-feeling in the whole of mankind would undoubtedly be easier if mankind were threatened with annihilation by an alien species. This certainly makes it more difficult to develop a we-group feeling relating to mankind as a whole. It also makes it more difficult, as we see, to recognize the fact that humanity is increasingly becoming the primary survival unit for all people as individuals and for all subgroups of mankind.

As far as can be seen, there is as yet no proper understanding of the implications of the present habitus in relation to the global situation. There now exist weapons that could destroy the majority of mankind and possibly the living conditions of mankind as a whole. This might give us cause to wonder, even in peacetime, whether a social habitus and a we-feeling attuned mainly to the single sovereign state are really adequate to the social situation in which people now live. Should we perhaps assume that here too the feelings, conscience and social habitus of individuals are lagging behind the social structures, and especially behind the level of integration that has emerged from the unplanned development of mankind?

What is certain is that as far as the relations between states are concerned we are continuing to live in the tradition of the sovereign princely state. We live in the age of technological war, with weapons that threaten the survival of mankind, as if inter-state relations could still be managed as they were in the time of Peter the Great or Louis XIV, when cannons were the most intimidating implements of warfare. As regards the internal affairs of the state, the relations between the rulers and the ruled have changed fundamentally. It is a part of the standard knowledge of our time that internal relations within a state can be changed in accordance with rules which are binding on all parties. Foreign policy, by contrast, is much less under the control of the ruled. In the inter-state sphere governments are still to a large extent absolute rulers, with a large measure of freedom of decision. This is apt to be concealed by the fact that they take a very limited number of members of parliament into their confidence in a manner convenient to them, passing them information in a suitably edited form. But in the name of state security this information is the privilege of a small circle whose members, even when they belong to different parties, are united by a strong we-feeling.

The discrepancy between the functional democratization of internal affairs and a management of foreign policy which is still in many ways absolutist, has far-reaching consequences. Governments and their secret services have a monopoly of knowledge about the actual or supposed military strength of rival states, knowledge from which the mass of the population is excluded in the name of national security. But it is not only in this respect that, even in parliamentary democracies, important features of absolutist foreign policy are perpetuated in international relations. The same applies to the way this policy finally serves the needs of the single sovereign state, now the nation state. A deliberate conditioning of the conscience which presents identification with the single state as the state citizen's highest duty plays its part in making arms races and the drift into war seem like forces beyond human control. The people in the confidence of the military, political and economic establishment are initiated into the real or supposed facts that enforce the next round of the arms build-up, but only they. The mass of the population are not in a position to test the selective information with which the government's policy is justified. They are not in a position to resist the appeal to their national loyalty. They are thus caught in a vicious circle which inevitably makes measures to secure the survival of their own group appear like measures threatening the survival of the opposing group, and vice versa.

The difficulty is that this tradition of inter-state relations, which has survived with little change from the days of the princely state until our own, brings with it, at the present stage of arms development, dangers that did not exist in the day of the musket. Despite all their assurances it is unlikely that the commanding generals are in a position to predict the consequences of the use of nuclear weapons. The experiences of the Chernobyl catastrophe suggest that the use of nuclear weapons will prove destructive not only for enemies but for friends and even one's own

population. We still plan and act within the traditional framework, as if the present weapons were still limited to destroying
the enemy's territory. That is certainly no longer the case. The
concept of humanity still has undertones of sentimental idealism.
This is hindering its development into a simple factual tool at a
time when radioactive clouds have travelled in a short period
from Russia to Britain. Depending on conditions, a hail of atomic
weapons on the United States could send radioactive clouds back
to Russia. It is difficult to imagine that the radioactive contamination of Europe would not bring with it lasting damage to Russia
and perhaps to China and even Japan, and conversely that the
contamination of Russia would not have the same effect on
Europe. To speak of humanity as the overarching survival unit
today is quite realistic. But the habitus of individuals, their
identification with limited sub-groups of mankind, particularly
single states, lags, to repeat the point, behind this reality. And
discrepancies of this kind are among the most dangerous structural features of the transitional stage at which we now find
ourselves.

All the same, there are already unambiguous signs that people
are beginning to identify with something beyond state borders,
that their we-group identity is moving towards the plane of
mankind. One of these signs is the importance that the concept of
human rights is gradually taking on. It is worthwhile at the end of
our study to look in more detail at what the demand for human
rights means. In its present form it includes the idea that limits
should be set on the omnipotence of the state in its treatment of
individual citizens. This resembles the way in which, at the earlier
transition from a lower to a higher plane of integration, limits
were set, by the relation to the higher level, on the power that
members of the lower level could wield over other members of
their association. The state claimed extensive powers over the
individuals forming it. In talking of human rights we say that the
individual as such, as a member of humanity, is entitled to rights
which limit the power of the state over the individual, regardless
of the laws of that state. These rights are generally thought to

include the individual's right to seek accommodation or work where he or she wishes, i.e. local or professional freedom of movement. Another well-known human right is protection of the individual against imprisonment by the state unless legitimized by public judicial procedures.

Perhaps it has not yet been stated clearly enough that human rights include the right of freedom from the use of physical force or even the threat of physical force, and the right to decline to use or threaten to use force in the service of another. The right to freedom for one's person or one's family from the use or threat of violence shows once again that the transition to a new, higher level of integration also involves a transition to a new position of the individual *vis-à-vis* his or her society. We have already seen that the development from clan and tribe to the state as the most important survival unit caused the individual to emerge from his previous lifelong pre-state associations. The transition to the primacy of the state in relation to clan and tribe meant an advance of individualization. As can be seen, the rise of mankind to become the dominant survival unit also marks an advance of individualization. As a human being an individual has rights that even the state cannot deny him or her. We are only at an early stage of the transition to the most comprehensive stage of integration, and the elaboration of what is meant by human rights is just beginning. But freedom from the use and threat of violence may so far have received too little attention as one of the rights which, in the course of time – and against the opposing tendencies of the state – will have to be asserted for the individual in the name of mankind.

Notes

1 Earlier, it might perhaps have been regarded as a law that reality-congruent concepts at a higher synthesis level are descended from ancestors representing a far lower level of synthesis (even though the languages of groups at a very early stage of development contain magic concepts at a very high

level of synthesis). But here the fact is registered simply as an observable regularity of conceptualizing processes, a regularity, moreover, that cannot be reversed. In addition, a process of this kind does not always operate in a straight line. A concept of unspecific generality can be narrowed down to become a specialist term for a particular group of facts without losing its generality. The concept of the individual, for example, that once referred to the uniqueness of each particular object, was narrowed in the course of time to denote only the uniqueness of a person.

2 We see here that, considered from the standpoint of process-sociology, "type" and "stage" are identical.

3 Looking back at the early stage of the discussion of the problem of individual and society, as presented in Part I of this volume, I find that the process-sociological approach does not emerge with sufficient force. I discover in the old text traces of the older sociological tradition in which problems relating to human beings were in some ways presented as if they were physical problems. The emancipation of the sociological mode of posing problems had already begun. But it was not carried through as rigorously as is possible at the present stage.

4 People talked, for example, of developing countries in order to avoid talking about less developed countries. And sociologists used the word "evolution" in order to avoid the stigmatized concept of development, thus concealing the difference between biological evolution and social development.

5 Cf., e.g., Norbert Elias, *Was ist Soziologie?*, Munich, 1972, pp. 132ff.

6 That one says "I" of oneself can easily seem the most spontaneous utterance of which a human being is capable. But this utterance is no different from others, for example, in the second and third persons, in that it too implies self-detachment. As is known, small children often first learn to refer to themselves in the same way as adults speak of them, e.g. by their names. The correct use of the term "I" often comes somewhat later, just because it requires the child to use linguistic forms in relation to himself which differ from those used by the parents in speaking about the child.

7 One of the general features of a powerful philosophical tradition extending from classical epistemology to the metaphysical philosophies of recent times, whether they are more transcendentally, existentially or phenomenologically inclined, is that its exponents take the isolated individual as their starting point. The plurality of human beings appears in philosophy as, at most, a plurality of identical special cases of general laws or regularities. Classical physics was the godfather of this tradition. Its modes of thought, in combination with theological ones, are reflected in it. An attempt by Leibniz to introduce the plurality of human beings into philosophy failed. The notion of the windowless monad was invincible. Hegel's attempt to bring social processes into philosophy also failed.

8 Jean-Paul Sartre, *Nausea*, translated by Lloyd Alexander, London, 1962, p 135

9 J P Toussaint, *La Salle de bain*, Paris, 1985, p 95

10 In Japan, however, the worker–employer relationship seems so far to have kept its lifelong character

11 What Max Weber presented as the Protestant Ethic was, in its early form in the seventeenth century, rather a symptom than the cause of a change in the social habitus of human beings – in this case mainly merchants who were rising or trying to rise socially – in the direction of greater individualization

12 Sociologists have tended in the past to regard the state as something that did not really come into the field of sociology Some of them may still incline towards this conviction An old intellectual tradition seems to be involved Society is usually regarded as the subject matter of sociology But the concept of society has undertones which make it seem as if state and society are not really compatible ideas The state appears as something extra-social, perhaps even something opposed to society Society itself, for its part, these undertones hint, is something extraneous to the state It has its own laws which are not the laws of the state and are not subject to the command of the government

Power struggles of an earlier epoch and a conceptual tradition reflecting them, survive in this subliminal antithesis between the concepts "state" and "society" In the eighteenth century the term society, as in the phrase "civil society", was indeed not infrequently used as an ideological code word, to express the idea that limits are set to the state's omnipotence If we pry behind these conceptual masks to see what personal, human problems were concealed behind these two seemingly impersonal, objective concepts, "civil society" and "the state", we soon catch sight of the answer Spokesmen of the rising middle class used concepts like "civil society" and finally "society" as intellectual weapons in their struggle with the upper class of their time, the princes and nobility who had a monopoly of state power The undertone of a difference, perhaps even an antithesis, between state and society, which gives the impression that the state is something extra-social, society something extraneous to the state, has not yet quite disappeared from the use of the terms There are many examples of power struggles of past epochs not merely giving new meanings to terms, but of these meanings lasting over long periods The anti-state connotations of the concept of society are just one of many examples They no doubt contributed to the fact that systematic sociological studies of states have been rare, until the current stage of state development going under the name of the "welfare" state, which has attracted the attention of sociologists

But perhaps the anti-state undertones of the concept of society would not have proved so durable had the ideological function not been allied to a discovery which was in part entirely objective and in that sense scientific. On one hand the change in the use of the term "society" in the eighteenth century, which found expression in concepts like that of civil society with its front against the upper classes and their state, certainly represented the growing self-confidence of rising bourgeois groups. But on the other it represented a growing insight into the autonomy of social processes and structures, the development of which often nullified the wishes and plans of the most powerful. The ideological legacy of the concept of society has undoubtedly caused much confusion. The anti-state front delayed for far too long the realization that states are social institutions with certain functions, and state-formation processes are social processes like any others. That we have until very recently had no comprehensive concept designating states like tribes as survival units, is a small example of the damage that an untested ideological legacy can cause in the use of concepts. But the same ideological attitude that for a considerable time banished states like other survival units from the field of sociology, at the same time opened the way to the realization that human societies are structures and processes of a peculiar kind. The confusing separation of society and state was the price that had to be paid for the discovery that the social co-existence of people throughout the world is a special realm that neither exists outside human individuals nor can be understood in terms of single human beings or reduced to them.

13 It is not difficult to find evidence of the personal problems, the demand for a change of social habitus, in a world in which the local mobility of human beings is greater than ever before. A growing number of people in all regions are caught up in this migration, whether with temporary or permanent goals. But even if they emigrate only temporarily, alone or with their families, to another country, they are clearly identifiable, not only for the people living there but for themselves, not just as individuals but as members of a particular group. That is not only the case because their passports label them such, but because their social habitus creates a specific kind of distance between them and members of the host country. People usually try to escape the difficulties of co-existence resulting from differences of social habitus by settling near members of their own group, i.e. people with the same social habitus.

In conjunction with such group settlements within host countries there are recurrent individual problems for members of the second or third generation of immigrant groups. They grow up in the shelter of their own groups. The example of their parents teaches them to take over the social habitus and the whole tradition of the group into their own personality structure. But at the same time they go to school in the host country. The language, manners, morals and customs of the host country also become built into their personality structures as if of their own accord. In this way tinder for personal and generational conflicts is produced. The parental models and the models of the host country, now the homeland, merge and conflict within the person of the individual. The ways individuals manage these model fusions or model conflicts no doubt vary widely. Some representatives of the second immigrant generation remain basically integrated into their origin-group, the group of their parents and relatives. The detachment of the second or third generation from their origin-group is difficult because the readiness and even the capacity of the established members of the host country to accept them is limited – of the host country, one must add, that is now the native country of the second and third immigrant generations. But recurrent difficulties and conflicts occur not only in the relation of these generations to members of the host country; they also occur with great regularity within the immigrant group and above all within the immigrant family. The problem of the sexual behaviour of girls is a particularly striking example.

14 I am grateful to Nico Stehr and Volker Meja for their information on this sect.

Editorial Afterword

Part I of the present volume was written in 1939 or slightly earlier; its publication in a Swedish journal planned at the time did not come about as the whole journal project failed to materialize. The text is reproduced here after the surviving original manuscript in the 1939 version, occasional (inconsistent) corrections and additions from various later periods being omitted. An important aid in establishing this version was a copy of the original manuscript made in Sweden in 1939; this was published by Nils Runeby of Stockholm University in 1983, with a historical-philological Foreword, as a duplicated typescript.

Part II was written, probably in several drafts, at a later time not yet established (1940s–50s). A few passages of this text are a direct revision of Part I.

Part III was written in winter 1986/7 for this edition.

Michael Schröter

Index

Lightning Source UK Ltd.
Milton Keynes UK
UKHW021020190619
344661UK00004B/44/P